To Rob and La SO-AVG-344
In grateful appreciation of
your service with Enoch. May
God bless your reading of this
book.
— Henry Christoph

A Token for Children

Being an exact account of the conversion,
holy and exemplary lives, and joyful deaths
of several young children in two parts.

by James Janeway
Minister of the Gospel

To which is added

A Token for the Children of New England

Or some examples of children in whom the fear of God was
remarkably budding before they died in several parts of
New England; published for the encouragement
of piety in other children.

by Cotton Mather

"Suffer the little children to come unto Me, and forbid them not:
for of such is the Kingdom of God." Mark 10:14

Soli Deo Gloria Publications
...for instruction in righteousness...

Soli Deo Gloria Publications
717 Liberty Avenue, Suite 2311
Pittsburgh, PA 15222
(412) 232-0866/FAX 232-0867

*

This edition of *A Token for Children* by James Janeway
has been retypeset and edited from the 1806 edition
published by Jane Aitken in Philadelphia,
and is © 1994 by Soli Deo Gloria.

.

This edition of *A Token for the Children of New England*
by Cotton Mather has been retypeset and edited
from the 1771 edition published by Z. Fowle in
Boston, and is © 1994 by Soli Deo Gloria.

*

ISBN 1-877611-76-X

Contents

A Token for Children

A Token for the Children
of New England

Contents

Foreword

A *Token for Children,* written by James Janeway in the 17th century, is designed for adults in the 21st century. If we contemporary "Christians" want to know what Christian experience is, we can do no better than to let these little children of centuries ago teach us. Cotton Mather's New England supplement, bound with Janeway, moves into the 18th century (Jonathan Edwards' Phoebe Bartlett in *Faithful Narrative of Surprising Conversions* is a good further supplement).

These little ones, ranging from 2 to 14, show the classical steps toward salvation beginning with correction and fear to struggle, regeneration, victory and, usually, supreme assurance of salvation. The experiences of many—on their deathbeds—full of confidence, consoling their grieving parents (often in the midst of great and prolonged pain), argue an abundant entrance into glory. Most of these children were reared in godly families but one was a London slum street boy, wonderfully converted through the charity of a godly friend.

The childrens' knowledge of Scripture was frightening. Most of the tots gave their days and nights, in health as well as sickness, to the study of the Bible. When they were not studying, they were witnessing to family and friends, as well as earnestly trying to correct and win the profane and worldly, young and old.

One omission in these narratives is surprising. I cannot remember a single allusion to infant baptism or

the covenant pertaining to children of believers. Many
modern covenantalists tend to asume election or conversion of such children. These children of James
Janeway and Cotton Matther knew they deserved to be
in hell unless the sovereign God they sought so zealously chose to give them a second birth from above.

Every modern Christian parent ought to buy and
study this book before making it required reading for
all his/her offspring. May the Lord whom commands
us to "suffer the little children to come unto Me," and
warns us that unless we come as little chldren we cannot enter His kingdom, BLESS YOU ALL.

Dr. John H. Gerstner
Ligonier, PA
January 1994

Introduction

Does it surprise you to discover that not only was this the most popular Puritan children's book, but that it continued to be influential for nearly 200 years after it was first published? We shall consider here its importance, background, and theological perspective on children's nurture.

There are two basic reasons for the republication and the reading of James Janeway's book *A Token for Children* and Cotton Mather's sequel to it, *A Token for the Children of New England.* First, there is the great historical importance of these books.

Given the definition of a children's book as one written for children (which excludes Bunyan's *Pilgrim's Progress*), *A Token for Children* may certainly be called the classic Puritan children's book, and has a good claim to the title of the classic Christian children's book of all time. During the 17th century, it was the most recommended book for children apart from the Bible[1]. What of its abiding usefulness, however? It was frequently reprinted in England and America throughout the 18th and much of the 19th centuries, with even an edition in the 20th century prior to this one. F.J. Harvey Darton, in his authoritative history of English Children's literature, said that James Janeway was "one who, after Bunyan, had the widest and longest popular-

---

[1] William Sloane, <u>Children's Books in England and American in the Seventeenth Century</u> (New York: King's Crown, 1955), p.44.

ity as the author of works read in English nurseries".[2]

Although this historical importance is noteworthy, a more significant reason for the republication and reading of *A Token for Children* is the biblical approach to children and children's literature that it represents. James Janeway recognizes that children are born dead in trespasses and sins. Thus, they need to be exhorted to repent and believe the gospel. For if they die without believing, they will spend eternity in hell. Janeway, therefore, powerfully and persuasively exhorts children to repent, believe the gospel, and live holy lives pleasing to God. Repentance, conversion, and holy lives are needed by children today just as much as they were by children in the 17th century.

The tragedy of our current Christian children's literature is that it differs little from that of the world, and the world is at enmity with God. Worldly children's literature is designed to amuse children and, thereby, distract them from seeking God. Modern critics regard Christian moral instruction as "marring" children's literature, and view evangelism in children's literature as annoying and antiquated. Robert Miner levels a typical criticism in his introduction to the 1977 edition of *A Token for Children*. He accuses Janeway of misinterpreting Christ's words, "Suffer the little children to come unto Me." As a result, he maintains, "generations of Puritan children came to believe that the gnashing of teeth was the true music of the spheres".[3] The attitude in general of the children's lit-

---

[2] F.J. Harvey Darton, Children's Books in England (New York: Cambridge University Press, 1960), p.54.

[3] Robert Miner in James Janeway's A Token for Children (New York:

erature critics seems to be that the more the gospel is disguised in a children's book, the better the book is (assuming the gospel is mentioned at all). This aversion to the gospel rather reminds one of John 3:19-20, "And men loved darkness rather than light, because their deeds were evil. For every one that doeth evil hateth the light, neither cometh to the light, lest his deeds should be reproved."

Most modern Christian children's writers depart from the world's guidelines only to the extent that they sneak in some moral lessons or, rarely, a few explicit words of the gospel, as they too write stories intended primarily to amuse children. There is a place for amusing children, but in biblical perspective that place cannot be the *pre-eminent* place in children's literature. Glorifying God must be the outstanding purpose. This is exactly the end that Janeway had in mind in writing *A Token for Children.*

But, some will argue, is not Janeway's book too sad for children? Is it not literally funerary religion, and does that honor the God whose prophet declared "the joy of the Lord is your strength," Nehemiah 8:10? Let us remember that God's Word must guide our understanding of the nature of both tragedy and joy. *A Token for Children* is thoroughly consistent with the joy that is the strength of God's people.

Janeway's brief masterpiece is by no means all sad. The children whose lives are recounted all die, but that is not the worst thing that can happen to a child. Dying without Christ is that worst thing, which happens to none of the children in Janeway's book. Coming to

Garland Publishing, Inc., 1977).

faith in Christ is really the best thing that can happen
to anyone; and, to get to that point, we often have to
suffer hardship and even anguish. The Bible says that
"we must through much tribulation enter into the
Kingdom of God," Acts 14:22. Yet again, with more direct application to the approach of Janeway and
Mather, "It is better to go to the house of mourning
than to go to the house of feasting: for that is the end
of all men; and the living will lay it to his heart. Sorrow
is better than laughter: for by the sadness of the countenance the heart is made better. The heart of the wise
is in the house of mourning; but the heart of fools is in
the house of mirth," Ecclesiastes 7:2-4. Biblical joy in
this life does not involve the absence of pain or mourning but a delight in God, His works, and His ways. This
joy in the Lord—something to which the regenerate
alone are entitled—is often intensified at a time of
trial, as James 1:2 shows, "Count it all joy when ye fall
into divers temptations." See also Matthew 5:12. Thus,
Janeway and Mather point us to the nature of true joy
and how to get it—by repentance and faith in God and
by submission and obedience to Him. If we are not the
fools described in Ecclesiastes 7:4, we do well to pay
close attention to them.

Who, then, was this James Janeway who wrote such
a significant book? He was the fourth son of the minister William Janeway, born in about 1636 at Lilley,
Hertfordshire. He graduated with a B.A. from Christ
Church, Oxford, in 1659. Although included in a list
of "ejected or silenced" ministers put out by the Act of
Uniformity in 1662, there seems to be no certain evidence that he functioned as a non-conformist preacher
in London until the plague year of 1665. He was then a

witness to a second great national calamity in London's Great Fire the following year. A meeting house was built for Janeway in 1672 in Rotherhithe, where he became very popular. Soldiers tore down the church building, and Janeway twice escaped arrest for his nonconformist preaching. He once was shot at, but the bullet merely passed through his hat. Janeway and his five brothers all died of tuberculosis before reaching age 40.[4] His familiarity with death, tribulation, and persecution would undoubtedly have served to concentrate his spiritual focus on matters close to the heart of God. When he died in 1674, he left a legacy of several spiritually rich publications, but *A Token for Children* has been the most enduring and the most popular.

That popularity extended to America as well as England. The book could not be imported fast enough from England to meet the demand for it, so Cotton Mather prepared an American edition in 1700, to which he appended a sequel of his own, *A Token for the Children of New England.* Cotton Mather (1663-1728), pastor of the Second (Old North) Church of Boston from 1683 to 1728, is still known today as a prominent figure in colonial New England, but is seldom pictured accurately. He took the Bible seriously and zealously sought to promote the cause of Christ generally, and help his own congregation particularly. He was regarded as a great scholar in England and Europe, as well as in New England. He was interested in history, science, and medicine in addition to theology strictly considered. He ultimately published over 400 works. His best known today is *Magnalia Christi Americana,* but

---

[4] F.J. Harvey Darton, <u>Children's Books in England</u>, p.57.

most popular in his own day was *Bonifacius: An Essay Upon the Good* [currently in production by Soli Deo Gloria]. His application of the Christian faith extended to family and children, of course, as evidenced by his sequel to Janeway's book.

How did such a scholar come to produce a book so similar to Janeway's? Mather also witnessed great national calamity. During King Philip's War (1675-1676), one out of every 16 New England men was killed by the Indians, and half the towns of New England suffered damage, with 12 completely destroyed. More importantly, Mather's personal life was marked by tragedy that has been compared with that of Job in the Bible. He lost his first wife in 1702 and his second in 1713. His third wife became mentally unbalanced and was a torment to him. He had 15 children by his first two wives, nine of whom died while very young, and only two of whom outlived him. Preaching at the funerals of children was something he did often, and it surely worked in him a desire to press the gospel home to children that they might be saved from hell. His *Token for the Children of New England* did just that.

Many of the subsequent American editions of Janeway's *A Token for Children* included Mather's sequel, particularly the editions published in New England. Janeway's book continued to be republished and widely read through the first half of the 19th century. But what happened at that time to make *A Token for Children* to fall from public favor? Wealth and life expectancy increased, and Augustine's adage demonstrated itself again that religion begat wealth and the daughter ate up the mother. Riches tend to breed complacency and formalism which are uncomfortable

in the presence of the searching exhortations made by
James Janeway and Cotton Mather. (Proverbs 30:9;
Deuteronomy 8:12-17; Matthew 19:24; Deuteronomy
32:15; and Matthew 6:19-21)

Nevertheless, we must mention here one particular
writer who greatly impacted orthodox views of the nature of children and, hence, materials suitable for their
spiritual instruction. That person was liberal theolo-
gian Horace Bushnell (1802-1876), whose writings di-
rectly attacked and, to a significant degree, overthrew
the biblical approach to children represented by
Janeway and Mather. Bushnell disapproved of "revival-
ism" and, instead, developed his own method for
church growth, which he elaborated in *Christian
Nurture*. Its basic idea is that "the child is to grow up a
Christian, and never know himself as being otherwise."

Christian Nurture was first published in 1847. A re-
vised and enlarged edition appeared in 1861. Bushnell's promoter, Luther Weigle, praised it as a classic of
American religious literature unrivaled except perhaps
by some of Jonathan Edwards' writings.[5] His statement
may be an exaggeration, but there is no question that
Christian Nurture was one of the most influential books
in American religious history. Sandford Fleming pro-
vides a detailed discussion of its influence in undoing
the biblical/Puritan approach to children—from a
liberal viewpoint—in chapter XVI of his *Children and
Puritanism*.

That such a rejection of original sin and total de-
pravity should sweep liberal circles is sad but not sur-

---

[5] Luther Weigle, in Horace Bushnell's Christian Nurture, (New Haven:
Yale University Press, 1967), p. xxxi.

prising. What is amazing is that many evangelicals such as Charles Hodge (1797-1878) expressed even qualified approval for the book.[6] With such support for *Christian Nurture*, Bushnell "became instrumental in inaugurating the modern era of religious education".[7] Bushnell's work questioned the wisdom and desirability of evangelizing children in professedly Christian homes, and hence deemed unnecessary—if not harmful—books like Janeway's, intended to evangelize such children. Bushnell thereby encouraged many to grow up in formalistic delusion, thinking themselves saved when they were not.

This is not to say that Horace Bushnell is responsible for all the evil in America today. It is to say that he had a much larger role in promoting the wickedly destructive force of theological liberalism than is usually realized today. The bitter fruits of Bushnell's works like *Christian Nurture* were certainly not desired or expected by those evangelicals who endorsed some of his ideas. They were likely influenced by the Victorian era's sentimentality about children, which blinded them to some degree to the liberalism implicit in Bushnell's chief book. Charles Hodge, for example, endorsed the view, common in his day even among evangelicals, that all infants dying in infancy would automatically go to heaven.[8] We must be careful to have our theology

---

[6] Elmer L. Towns, ed., A History of Religious Educators (Grand Rapids: Baker Book House, 1975), pp. 284-285.

[7] J.I. Neve and O.W. Heick, A History of Christian Thought (Philadelphia: The Muhelnberg Press, 1946), II, 287.

[8] Charles Hodge, Systematic Theology (Grand Rapids: Wm. B. Eerdmans, 1975), I, 26-27.

guide our emotions and not vice versa. The great Presbyterian preacher, Gilbert Tennent (1703-1764), reminds us, "The passions make poor guides but notwithstanding good servants."[9] Our natural affection for our children, in particular, must run in biblical channels.

How are we to so order our affection for our children in a biblical way? Studying with *A Token for Children* and *A Token for the Children of New England,* with the prayer that God would use these books to bring about our children's salvation, is an excellent start. I would heartily recommend that you begin with Janeway's powerful prefaces.

Henry Christoph
Boonton, NJ
February 1994

---

[9] Gilbert Tennent, <u>A Persuasive to the Right Use of the Passions in Religion</u> (Philadelphia: W. Dunlap, 1760), p.5.

A Token
for Children

Being an exact account of the conversion,
holy and exemplary lives, and joyful
deaths of several young children
in two parts.

by

James Janeway

A Preface Containing Directions to Children

You may now hear, my dear lambs, what other good children have done, and remember how they wept and prayed by themselves; how earnestly they cried out for an interest in the Lord Jesus Christ. May you now read how dutiful they were to their parents, how diligent at books, how ready to learn the Scripture and their catechisms. Can you forget what questions they were inclined to ask, how much they feared a lie, how much they abhorred naughty company, how holy they lived, how dearly they were loved, how joyfully they died?

But tell me, my dear children, and tell me truly, do you do as much as these children did? Did you ever see your miserable state by nature? Did you ever get by yourself and weep for sin, and pray for grace and pardon? Did you ever go to your father and mother, master or mistress, and beg them to pity you, to pray for you, and to teach you what you shall do to be saved, what you shall do to get Christ, heaven, and glory? Do you love to be taught good things? Come, tell me truly, my dear child, for I would gladly do what I possibly can to keep you from falling into everlasting fire. I would gladly have you be one of those little ones which Christ will take into His arms and bless.

How do you spend your time? Is it in play and idleness, as with wicked children? Dare you take God's name in vain, or swear, or tell a lie? Dare you do anything which your parents forbid you, and neglect to do what they command you? Do you dare to run up and down upon the Lord's Day? Or do you keep in to read your book and to learn what your good parents command you? What do you say, child? Which of these two sorts are you? Let me talk a little with you and ask a few questions.

1. Were not these children sweet children who feared God and were dutiful to their parents? Did not their fathers and mothers, and everybody who fears God, love them and praise them? What do you think is become of them now that they are dead and gone? Why, they are gone to heaven and are singing hallelujahs with the angels. They see glorious things, and are having nothing but joy and pleasure. They shall never sin anymore, shall never be chastened anymore, they shall never be sick or in pain anymore.

2. And would you not have your father's love, your mother's commendation, your master's good word? Would you not have God and Christ love you? Would you not gladly go to heaven when you die and live with your godly parents in glory and be happy forever?

3. Where do you think those children go when they die who will not do what they are bid, but play the truant, and lie, and speak naughty words, and break the Sabbath? Where do such children go, do you think? Why, I will tell you—they who lie must go with their father the devil into everlasting burning. They who never pray, God will pour out His wrath upon them. And, when they beg and pray in hellfire, God will not forgive them, but there they must lie forever.

4. And are you willing to go to hell to be burned

with the devil and his angels? Would you be in the same condition as naughty children? O hell is a terrible place that's a thousand times worse than whipping. God's anger is worse than your father's anger, and are you willing to anger God? O child, this is most certainly true, that all who are wicked and die so must be turned into hell. And if any are once there, there is no coming out again.

5. Would you not do anything in the world rather than be thrown into hellfire? Would you not do anything in the world to get Christ, grace, and glory?

6. Well, now, what will you do? Will you read this book a little because your good mother will make you do it, and because it is a new book? But, as soon as you have done with it, will you run away to play and never think of it?

7. How are you now affected, poor child, in the reading of this book? Have you shed even a tear since you began reading? Have you been by yourself upon your knees, begging that God would make you like these blessed children? Or are you as you used to be, as careless, foolish, disobedient, and wicked as ever?

8. Did you never hear of a little child that died? And, if other children die, why may not you be sick and die? And what will you do then, child, if you should have no grace in your heart, and be found like other naughty children?

9. How do you know but that you may be the next child that may die? And where are you then, if you are not God's child?

10. Will you tarry any longer, my dear child, before you run into your chamber and beg God to give you Christ for your soul, that you may not be undone

forever? Will you get immediately into a corner and weep and pray? I think I see one pretty lamb beginning to weep, and think of getting by himself, and will, as well as he can, cry unto the Lord to make him one of those little ones who go into the kingdom of heaven. I think there stands a sweet child, and there another, who are resolved for Christ and heaven. I think that little boy looks as if he had a mind to learn good things. I think I hear one saying, "Well, I never will tell a lie anymore. I will never keep any naughty boy's company anymore. They will teach me to swear, and they will speak naughty words. They do not love God! I'll learn my catechism and get my mother to teach me to pray and will go weep and cry to Christ and will not be quiet until the Lord has given me grace." O that's my brave child, indeed!

11. But will you not quickly forget your promise? Are you resolved, by the strength of Christ, to be a good child? Are you indeed? Nay, but are you indeed? Consider, dear child, God calls you to remember your Creator in the days of your youth. He takes it kindly when little ones come to Him, and He loves them dearly. And godly people, especially parents, masters, and mistresses, have no greater joy than to see their children walking in the way of truth.

12. Now tell me, my pretty, dear child, what will you do? Shall I make you a book? Shall I pray for you and entreat for you? Shall your good mother weep over you? And will you not make us all glad by turning quickly to the Lord? Shall Christ tell you that He will love you, and will you not love Him? Will you strive to be like these children? I am persuaded that God intends to do good to the souls of some little children

by these papers because He has laid it so much upon my heart to pray for them, and over these papers, and, through mercy I have already experienced that something of this nature has not been in vain.

I shall give a word of direction, and so leave you.

1. Take heed of what you know is naughty, like lying. O that is a grievous fault indeed. And so are naughty words and taking the Lord's name in vain and playing upon the Lord's Day and keeping bad company and playing with ungodly children. But, if you go to school with such, tell them that God will not love them but that the devil will have them if they continue to be so naughty.

2. Do what your father and mother bid you cheerfully, and take heed of doing anything they forbid you.

3. Be diligent in reading the Scripture and learning your catechism. And, what you do not understand, be sure to ask the meaning of.

4. Think a little, sometimes, by yourself about God, heaven, your soul, and what Christ came into the world for.

5. And, if you have no great mind to do thus but would rather be at play, then think, "Why is it that I do not care for good things? Is this like one of God's dear children? I am afraid I am not God's child. I feel I do not love to come unto Him. O what shall I do? Either I will be God's child or the devil's. O what shall I do! I would not be the devil's child for anything in the world!"

6. Then go to your father and mother, or some good person, and ask them what you shall do to be God's child. Tell them that you are not afraid, and that

you cannot be contented until you have gotten the love of God.

7. Get by yourself into the chamber or some private place, fall upon your knees, weep and mourn, and tell Christ that you are afraid that He does not love you, but that you would gladly have His love. Beg Him to give you His grace and pardon for your sins, and that He would make you His child. Tell God that you do not care who doesn't love you if God will but love you. Say to Him, "Have you not a blessing for me, Thy poor little child? Father, hast Thou not a blessing for me, even for me? O give me an interest in Christ! O let me not be undone for ever!"

Thus beg, as for your lives, and do not be contented until you have an answer. And do this every day with as much earnestness as you can, twice a day at least.

8. Give yourself up to Christ. Say, "Dear Jesus, Thou didst bid that little children should be suffered to come unto Thee and, Lord, I am come as well as I can. I would gladly be Thy child. Take my heart and make it humble and meek, sensible and obedient. I give myself unto Thee, dear Jesus. Do what Thou wilt with me, so that Thou wilt but love me and give me Thy grace and glory."

9. Get acquainted with godly people, and ask them good questions. Endeavor to love their talk.

10. Labor to get a dear love for Christ. Read the history of Christ's sufferings, and ask the reason of His sufferings. Never be content until you see your need of Christ and the excellency and use of Christ.

11. Hear the most powerful ministers, and read the most searching books. Get your father to buy you such

as are serious and instructive.

12. Resolve to continue in well-doing all your days. Then you shall be one of those sweet little ones that Christ will take into His arms, and bless, and give kingdom crowns and glory to. And now, dear children, I have done. I have written to you. I have prayed for you, but what you will do I cannot tell. O children, if you love me, if you love your parents, if you love your souls, if you would escape hellfire, and if you would live in heaven when you die, go and do as these good children. And that you may be your parent's joy, your country's honor, and live in God's fear, and die in His love, is the prayer of your dear friend,

James Janeway

Preface to Parents and Teachers

To all Parents, School-Masters, and School-Mistresses, or any who are concerned with the education of children.

Dear Friends,

I have often thought that Christ speaks to you as Pharaoh's daughter did to Moses' mother, "Take this child and nurse it for me." Consider what a precious jewel is committed to your charge, what an advantage you have to show your love to Christ, to stock the next generation with noble plants, and what a joyful account you may make if you are faithful. Remember, souls, Christ and grace cannot be overvalued. I confess you have some disadvantages, but let that only excite your diligence. The salvation of souls, the commendation of your Master, the greatness of your reward and everlasting glory, will pay for all.

Remember, the devil is hard at work. Wicked ones are industrious, and a corrupt nature is a rugged, knotty piece to hew. Do not be discouraged. I am almost as much afraid of your laziness and unfaithfulness as anything. Go to work in good earnest, and who knows but that rough stone may prove to be a pillar in the temple of God?

In the name of the living God, as you will answer it

shortly at his bar, I command you to be faithful in instructing and catechizing your young ones. If you think I am too peremptory, I pray, read the command from my Master Himself in Deuteronomy 6:7. Is not the duty clear? And do you dare neglect so direct a command? Are the souls of your children of no value? Are you willing that they should be brands of hell? Are you indifferent as to whether they are damned or saved? Shall the devil run away with them without control? Will you not use your utmost endeavor to deliver them from the wrath to come?

You see that they are not subjects incapable of the grace of God. Whatever you think of them, Christ does not slight them. They are not too little to die, nor are they too little to go to hell. They are not too little to serve their Master, nor too little to go to heaven. "For of such is the kingdom of God." And will not a possibility of their conversion and salvation put you upon the greatest diligence to teach them? Or are Christ and heaven and salvation small things with you? If they are, then indeed I have done with you. But, if they are not, I beseech you to lay about you with all your might. The devil knows your time is going apace. It will be too late soon.

Therefore, what you do, do quickly, and do it with all your might. O pray, pray, pray, and live holily before them, and take some time daily to speak a little to your children one by one about their miserable condition by nature. I knew a child who was converted by this sentence from a godly school-mistress in the country, "Every mother's child of you is by nature a child of wrath."

Put your children upon learning their catechism,

and the Scripture, and getting to pray and weep by themselves after Christ. Take heed of their company. Take heed of pardoning a lie. Take heed of letting them misspend the Sabbath. Put them, I beseech you, upon imitating these sweet children. Let them read this book over a hundred times. Observe how they are affected. Ask them what they think of those children, and whether they would not be such?

Follow what you do with earnest cries to God, and be in travail to see Christ formed in their souls. I have prayed for you. I have often prayed for your children, and I love them dearly. And I have prayed over these papers that God would strike in with them and make them effectual to the good of their souls. Encourage your children to read this book and lead them to improve by it. What is presented is faithfully taken from experienced, solid Christians, some of them no way related to the children, who themselves were eye and ear witnesses of God's works of wonder; or from my own knowledge; or from reverend, godly ministers, and from persons who are of unspotted reputation for holiness, integrity, and wisdom. Several passages are taken verbatim in writing from their dying lips.

I may add many other excellent examples, if I have any encouragement in this piece, which the author has done in the second part. That the young generation may be far more excellent than this is the prayer of one that dearly loves little children.

James Janeway

A Token
for Children

Example 1

Of one eminently converted between eight and nine years old, with an account of her life and death.

Miss Sarah Howley, when she was between eight and nine years old, was carried by her friends to hear a sermon, where the minister preached upon Matthew 11:13, "My yoke is easy, and My burden is light," in the applying of which Scripture the child was mightily awakened, and made deeply sensible of the condition of her soul and her need of Christ. She wept bitterly to think what a case she was in, and went home and got by herself into a chamber and, upon her knees, wept and cried to the Lord as well as she could, which might easily be perceived by her eyes and countenance.

She was not contented at this, but she got her little brother and sister into a chamber with her and told them of their condition by nature, and wept over them, and prayed with them and for them.

After this, she heard another sermon upon Proverbs 29:1, "He that, being often reproved, hardeneth his heart, shall suddenly be destroyed, and that without remedy," at which she was more affected than before, and was so exceeding solicitous about her soul that she spent a great part of the night in weeping and praying, and could scarcely take any rest day or night for some time together, desiring with all her soul to escape from everlasting flames and to get an interest in the Lord Jesus. O what should she do for Christ? What should she do to be saved?

She gave herself much to attending upon the Word preached, and still continued very tender under it, greatly savoring what she heard.

She was very much in secret prayer, as might easily be perceived by those who listened at her chamber door, and was usually very importunate, full of tears.

She could scarcely speak of sin, or be spoken to, but her heart was ready to melt.

She spent much time in reading the Scripture and a book called *The Best Friend in the Worst of Times* [the subtitle of Janeway's *Heaven Upon Earth*], by which the work of God was much promoted upon her soul, and was much directed by it how to get acquaintance with God, especially towards the end of that book. Another book that she was much delighted with was Mr. [George] Swinnock's *Christian Man's Calling*,[1] and by

---

[1] George Swinnock (1627-1673), Puritan non-conformist pastor and author, published *The Christian Man's Calling* between 1661 and 1665. It is included in the five volumes of his works recently reprinted by the

Example 1   3

this she was taught in this measure to make religion her business. *The Spiritual Bee* [by Nicholas Horsman] was a great companion of hers.

She was exceedingly dutiful to her parents, very loath to grieve them in the least. If she had at any time (which was very rare) offended them, she would weep bitterly.

She abhorred lying, and allowed herself in no known sin.

She was very conscientious in spending of time, and hated idleness, and spent her whole time either in praying, reading, or instructing her little brothers, and working at her needle, at which she was very ingenious.

When she was at school, she was eminent for her diligence, teachableness, meekness and modesty, speaking little. But, when she did speak, it was usually spiritual.

She continued in this course of religious duties for some years together.

When she was about 14 years old, she broke a vein in her lungs (as is supposed), and often spit blood. She recovered a little but had several dangerous relapses.

At the beginning of last January, she was taken very bad again, in which sickness she was in great distress of soul. When she was first taken, she said, "O mother, pray, pray, pray for me, for Satan is so busy that I cannot pray for myself. I see I am undone without Christ and a pardon! O I am undone to all eternity!"

Her mother, knowing how serious she had been formerly, wondered a little that she should be in such agonies, upon which her mother asked her what sin it

Banner of Truth Trust.

was that was so burdensome to her spirits. "O mother, it is not any particular sin of omission or comission that sticks so close to my conscience as the sin of my nature. Without the blood of Christ, that will damn me."

Her mother asked her what she should pray for her. She answered, "That I may have a saving knowledge of sin and Christ, and that I may have an assurance of God's love to my soul." Her mother asked her why she spoke so little to the minister who had come to her. She answered that it was her duty, with patience and silence, to learn from him. And it was exceedingly painful for her to speak to anyone.

One time, when she fell into a fit, she cried out, "O I am going, I am going! But what shall I do to be saved? Sweet Lord Jesus, I will lie at Thy feet and, if I perish, it shall be at the fountain of Thy mercy."

She was much afraid of presumption and dreaded a mistake in the matters of her soul. She would often be putting up ejaculations to God to deliver her from deceiving herself. To instance in one, "Great and mighty God, give me faith, and true faith, Lord, that I may not be a foolish virgin, having a lamp and no oil."

She would, many times, be laying hold upon the promises, and plead them in prayer. That passage in Matthew 11:28-29 was much on her tongue and was no small relief to her spirit. How many times would she cry out, "Lord, hast Thou not said, 'Come unto Me, all ye that are weary and heavy laden, and I will give you rest.'?"

Another time, her father bid her be of good cheer because she was going to a better Father, at which she was much affected and said, "But how do I know that? I

Example 1   5

am a poor sinner who lacks assurance. O for assurance!" It was still her great note, "O for assurance!" This was her great, earnest, and constant request to all who came to her, to beg assurance for her. And, poor heart, she would look with so much eagerness upon them as if she desired nothing in the world so much as that they would pity her, and help her with their prayers. Never was a poor creature more earnest for anything than she was for assurance and the light of God's countenance. O the piteous moan that she would make! O the agonies her soul was in!

Her mother asked her how she would live if God should spare her. "Truly, mother," said she, "we have such base hearts that I cannot tell. We are apt to promise great things when we are sick, but when we are recovered, we are as ready to forget ourselves and turn again to folly. But I hope I shall be more careful of my time and my soul than I have been."

She was full of natural affection to her parents and very careful lest her mother should be tired out with much watching. Her mother said, "How shall I bear parting with you, when I have scarcely dried my eyes for your brother?" She answered, "The God of love will support and comfort you. It is but a little while and we shall meet in glory, I hope." She, being very weak, could only speak a little. Therefore, her mother said, "Child, if you have any comfort, lift up your head," which she did.

The Lord's day before that in which she died, a kinsman of hers came to see her. Being asked whether she knew him, she answered, "Yea, I know you, and I desire that you would learn to know Christ. You are young, but you do not know how soon you may die;

and O to die without Christ is a fearful thing. O redeem time! O time, time, time, precious time!"

Being requested by him not to spend herself, she said she would gladly do all the good she could while she lived, and when she was dead too, if possible. Upon which account she desired that a sermon might be preached at the funeral concerning the preciousness of time. O that young ones would now remember their Creator!

Some ministers who came to her begged with earnestness that the Lord would be pleased to give her some token for good so that she might go off triumphing. And requests of the same nature were sent to several churches.

After she had long waited for an answer of their prayers, she said, "Well, I will venture my soul upon Christ."

She carried it with wonderful patience. Yet she would often pray that the Lord would give her more patience, which the Lord answered to astonishment. For, considering the pains and agonies that she was in, her patience was next to a wonder. "Lord, Lord, give me patience," she said, "that I might not dishonor Thee."

Upon Thursday, after long waiting, great fears, and many prayers, when all her friends thought she had been past speaking, to the astonishment of all her friends, she broke forth thus with a very audible voice and cheerful countenance, "Lord, Thou hast promised that whosoever comes unto Thee, Thou wilt in no wise cast out. Lord, I come unto Thee, and surely Thou wilt in no ways cast me out. O sweet! O so glorious is Jesus. O I have the sweet and glorious Jesus; He is sweet, He

Example 1   7

is sweet, He is sweet! O the admirable love of God in
sending Christ! O free grace to a poor, lost creature!"
  And thus she ran on repeating many of these things
a hundred times over. But her friends were so astonished to see her in this divine rapture, and to hear
such gracious words, and her prayers and desires satisfied, that they could not write a quarter of what she
spoke.
  When her soul was thus ravished with the love of
Christ, and her tongue so highly engaged in the mag-
nifying of God, her father, brothers and sisters, with
others of the family, were called, to whom she spoke
particularly as her strength would give her leave. She
gave her Bible as a legacy to one of her brothers, and
desired him to use that well for her sake, and added to
him and the rest, "O make use of time to get Christ for
your souls. Spend no time in running up and down in
playing. O get Christ for your souls while you are
young! Remember now your Creator before you come
to a sick bed. Do not put off this great work till then,
for then you will find it a hard work indeed. I know by
experience that the devil will tell you, 'It is time
enough, and you are young. What need do you have to
be in such haste? You will have time enough when you
are old.' But there stands one (meaning her grandmother) who stays behind, and I, who am young, am
going before her. O therefore make your calling and
election sure while you are in health. But I am afraid
this will be but one night's trouble to your thoughts.
But, remember, these are the words of a dying sister. O
if you knew how good Christ was! O if you had but one
taste of His sweetness, you would rather go to Him a
thousand times than stay in this wicked world! I would

not for 10,000 and 10,000 worlds part with my interest in Christ. O how happy am I that I am going to everlasting joys! I would not go back again for 20,000 worlds, and will you not strive to get an interest in Christ?"

After this, looking upon one of her father's servants, she said, "What shall I do? What shall I do at the great day, when Christ shall say to me, 'Come thou blessed of My Father, inherit the kingdom prepared for thee; and shall say to the wicked, Go thou cursed into the lake that burns forever?' " What a grief is it for me to think that I shall see any of my friends, who I knew upon earth, turned into that lake that burns forever! O that word 'forever,' remember that word 'forever.' I speak these words to you, but they are nothing unless God speaks to you too. O pray, pray, pray that God would give you grace." And then she prayed, "O Lord, finish Thy work upon their souls. It will be my comfort to see you in glory, but it will be your everlasting happiness."

Her grandmother told her she spent herself too much. She said, "I do not care about that if I can do any soul good." O with what vehemence she spoke, as if her heart were in every word she spoke.

She was full of divine sentences, and nearly her entire discourse from the first to the last in the time of her sickness was about her soul, Christ's sweetness, and the souls of others—in a word, it was like a continual sermon.

Upon Friday, after she had had such lively discoveries of God's love, she was exceedingly desirous to die and cried out, "Come, Lord Jesus, come quickly. Conduct me to Thy tabernacle. I am a poor creature

Example 1   9

without Thee. But, Lord Jesus, my soul longs to be with
Thee. O when shall it be? Why not now, dear Jesus?
Come, Lord Jesus, come quickly. But why do I speak
thus? Thy time, dear Lord, is the best. O give me patience!"

Upon Saturday, she spoke very little, being very
drowsy, yet now and then she dropped these words,
"How long, sweet Jesus? Finish Thy work, come away,
sweet dear Lord Jesus. Come quickly. Sweet Lord, help.
Come away, now, now, dear Jesus, come quickly. Good
Lord, give me patience to wait Thy appointed time.
Lord Jesus, help me, help me, help me." Thus, it was at
several times (when out of her sleep), for she was
asleep the greatest part of the day.

Upon the Lord's Day, she scarcely spoke anything,
but much desired that notes of thanksgiving might be
sent to those who had formerly been praying for her,
that they might help her to praise God for that full assurance that He had given her of His love. And she
seemed to be much swallowed up with the thoughts of
God's free love to her soul. She often commended her
spirit into the Lord's hands, and the last words she was
heard to speak were these, "Lord, help. Lord Jesus,
help. Dear Jesus, blessed Jesus."

And thus, upon the Lord's Day, between nine and
ten o'clock in the forenoon, she slept sweetly in Jesus,
and began an everlasting Sabbath, February 19, 1670.

Example 2

Of a child who was admirably affected with the things of God, when he was between two and three years old; with a brief account of his life and death.

A certain little child, when he could not speak plainly, would be crying after God, and was greatly desirous to be taught good things.

He could not endure to be put to bed without family prayer, but would put his parents upon duty and would with much devotion kneel down and with great patience and delight continue till duty was at an end without the least expression of being weary. And he seemed never so well-pleased as when he was engaged in prayer.

He could not be satisfied with family prayer but would often be upon his knees by himself in one corner or another.

He was much delighted to hear the Word of God either preached or read.

He loved to go to school that he might learn something of God. He would observe and take great notice of what he read, and come home and speak of it with much affection. And he would rejoice in his book and say, "O mother! I have had a sweet lesson today, will you please give me leave to fetch my book that you may hear it?"

As he grew up, he was more and more affected with the things of another world—so that, if we had not

Example 2   11

received our information from one who is of undoubted fidelity, it would seem incredible.

He quickly learned to read the Scriptures and would with great reverence, tenderness, and groans, read till tears and sobs were ready to hinder him.

When he was at secret prayer, he would weep bitterly.

He was inclined, oftentimes, to complain of the naughtiness of his heart, and seemed to be much grieved for the corruption of his nature, and for actual sin.

He had a vast understanding in the things of God, even to a wonder, for one of his age.

He was much troubled for the wandering of his thoughts in duty, and that he could not keep his heart always fixed upon God and the work he was about, nor his affections constantly raised.

He kept a watch over his heart, and observed the workings of his soul. He would complain that they were so vain and foolish and so little busied about spiritual things.

As he grew up, he grew daily in knowledge and experience. His carriage was so heavenly, and his discourse so excellent and experimental, that it made those who heard it astonished.

He was exceedingly importunate with God in prayer, and would so plead with Him, and use such arguments in prayer, that one would think it impossible that it should enter into the heart of a child. He would beg and expostulate and weep so that sometimes it could not be kept from the ears of neighbors. One of the next house was forced to cry out, "The prayers and tears of that child will sink me to hell, because by it he condemns my neglect of prayer and my slight performance of it."

He was very fearful of wicked company, and would often beg God to keep him from it, and that he might never be pleased in those who took delight in displeasing God. When he was at any time hearing their wicked words, taking the Lord's name in vain, or swearing, or any filthy words, it would even make him tremble and ready to go home and weep.

He abhorred lying with all his soul.

When he had committed any fault, he was easily convinced of it and would get in some corner and secret place and with tears beg pardon of God and strength against such a sin. He had a friend who often watched him, and listened at his chamber door, from whom I received this narrative.

When he had been asked whether he would commit such a sin again, he would never promise absolutely, because he said his heart was wicked. But he would weep and say that he hoped, by the grace of God, that he would not.

When he was left at home upon the Sabbath days, he would be sure not to spend any part of the day in idleness and play but be busied in praying, reading the Bible, and getting his catechism.

When other children were playing, he would many a time and often be praying.

One day, a certain person was discoursing with him about the nature, offices, and excellency of Christ, and that He alone can satisfy for our sins and merit everlasting life for us, and about other great mysteries of redemption. He seemed savingly to understand them, and was greatly delighted with the discourse.

Example 2   13

On speaking concerning the resurrection of the body, he acknowledged it, but that the same weak body that was buried in the churchyard should be raised again he thought very strange. But with admiration, he yielded that nothing was impossible to God. That very day he was taken sick unto death.

A friend of his asked him whether he was willing to die when he was first taken sick. He answered no, because he was afraid of his state as to another world. "Why, child," said the other, "you prayed for a new heart, for a humble and sincere heart, and I have heard you. Did you not pray with your heart?"

"I hope I did," he said.

Not long after, the same person asked him again whether he was willing to die. He answered, "Now I am willing, for I shall go to Christ."

One asked him what should become of his sister, if he should die and leave her. He answered, "The will of the Lord be done."

He grew weaker and weaker still, but carried it with a great deal of sweetness and patience, waiting for his change, and at last cheerfully committed his spirit unto the Lord, calling upon His name and saying, "Lord Jesus, Lord Jesus," in whose bosom he sweetly slept, dying, as I remember, when he was about six years old.

Example 3

Of a little girl who was wrought upon when she was between four and five years old, with some account of her holy life and triumphant death.

Mary A., when she was between four and five years old, was greatly affected in hearing the Word of God, and became very solicitous about her soul and everlasting condition. She wept bitterly to think what would become of her in another world, asking many questions concerning God, Christ, and her own soul. So then this little Mary, before she was five years old, seemed to mind the one thing needful and to choose the better part, and sat at the feet of Christ many a time, and often with tears.

She was inclined to be much in secret prayer. And, many times, she came off from her knees with tears.

She would choose such times and places for secret prayer as might render her less observed by others, and endeavored what she possibly could to conceal what she was doing when she was engaged in secret duty.

She was greatly afraid of hypocrisy, and of doing any thing to be seen of men and get commendation and praise. When she had heard one of her brothers saying that he had been by himself at prayer, she rebuked him sharply and told him how little such prayers were likely to profit him, and that it was little to his praise to pray like a hypocrite and be glad that any should know what he had been doing.

Example 3   15

Her mother, full of sorrow after the death of her husband, was asked by this child why she wept so exceedingly. Her mother answered that she had cause enough to weep because her father was dead. "No, dear mother," said the child, "you have no occasion to weep so much, for God is a good God still to you."

She was a dear lover of faithful ministers. One time, after she had been hearing Mr. Whitaker, she said, "I love that man dearly for the sweet words that he speaks concerning Christ."

Her book was her delight, and what she read she loved to make her own, and cared not for passing over what she learned without extraordinary observations and understanding. Many times she was so strangely affected in reading the Scriptures that she would burst out into tears and would hardly be pacified, so greatly was she taken with Christ's sufferings, the zeal of God's servants, and the danger of a natural estate.

She would complain, often times, of the corruption of her nature and the hardness of her heart, that she could repent no more thoroughly and be no more humble and grieved for her sins against a good God. And when she complained thus, it was with abundance of tears.

She was greatly concerned for the souls of others, grieved to think of the miserable condition that they were in upon this account. When she could, she would be putting in some thing concerning Christ. But above all, she would do what she could to draw the hearts of her brethren and sisters after Christ. And there were no small hopes that her example and good counsel prevailed with some of them when they were very young to get into corners to pray and ask very gracious questions about the things of God.

She was very conscientious in keeping the Sabbath, spending the whole time either in reading, praying, learning her catechism, or teaching her brothers and sisters. One time when she was left at home upon the Lord's Day, she got some other children together with her brothers and sisters. Instead of playing (as other naughty children used to do), she told them that this was the Lord's Day, and that they ought to remember that day to keep it holy. And then she told them how it was to be spent in religious exercises all the day long, except so much as was to be taken up in the works of necessity and mercy. Then she prayed with them herself and, among other things, begged that the Lord would give grace and wisdom to those little children, that they might know how to serve Him, as one of those little ones in the company with her told her afterwards.

She was a child of great tenderness and compassion to all, full of kindness and pity. Whom she could not help, she would be ready to weep over, especially if she saw her mother at any time troubled. She would quickly make her sorrows her own, and weep for her and with her.

When her mother had been somewhat solicitous about any wordly thing, she would, if she could possibly, put her off from her care one way or another. One time she told her, "O mother, the grace of God is better than that (meaning something her mother wanted). I would rather have the grace and love of Christ than anything in the world."

This child was often musing and busied in the thoughts of her everlasting work. Witness that strange

Example 3 17

question, "O what are they doing which are already in heaven?" And she seemed to be greatly desirous to be among them who were praising, loving, delighting in God, and serving Him without sin. Her language about spiritual matters made many excellent Christians to stand amazed, judging it scarcely to be paralleled.

She took great delight in reading the Scripture, and part of it was more sweet to her than her appointed food. She would get several choice Scriptures by heart, and discourse of them favorably, and apply them suitably.

She was not altogether a stranger to other good books but would read them with much affection. And where she might, she noted the books particularly, observing what in the reading most warmed her heart, and she was ready upon occasion to improve it.

One time, a woman coming into the house in a great passion spoke of her condition as if none were like hers, and it would never be otherwise. The child said that it would be a strange thing to say when it is night that it will never be day again.

At another time, a near relation of hers, being in some straits, made some complaints, to whom she said, "I have heard Mr. Carter say, 'A man may go to heaven without a penny in his purse, but not without grace in his heart.' "

She had an extraordinary love to the people of God, and when she saw any who she thought feared the Lord, her heart would leap for joy.

She loved to be much by herself and would be greatly grieved if she were at any time deprived of a convenience for secret prayer. She could not live without constant address to God in secret and was not a little pleased when she could go into a corner to pray and weep.

She was much in praising God, and seldom or never complained of anything but sin.

She continued in this course of praying and praising God, and great dutifulness and sweetness to her parents and those who taught her anything. She greatly encouraged her mother while she was a widow, and desired that the absence of a husband might, in some measure, be made up by the dutifulness and holiness of a child. She studied all the ways that could be to make her mother's life comfortable.

When she was between 11 and 12 years old, she sickened in which time she carried it with admirable patience, and did what she could with Scripture arguments to support and encourage her relations to part with her, as she was going to glory, and to prepare themselves to meet her in a blessed eternity.

She was not sick many days before she became dangerous, of which she was sensible and rejoiced that she was now going quickly to Christ. She called to her friends and said, "Do not be troubled, for I know I am one of the Lord's own."

One asked her how she knew that, and she answered, "The Lord has told me that I am one of His dear children." And thus she spoke with a holy confidence in the Lord's love to her soul. She was not in the least daunted when she spoke of her death, but seemed greatly delighted in the apprehension of her nearness to her father's house. And it was not long before she was filled with joy unspeakable in believing.

When she lay a-dying, her mother came to her and told her she was sorry that she had reproved and

Example 3   19

corrected so good a child so often. "O mother," she said, "do not speak this way. I bless God now that I am dying for your reproofs and corrections too, for, it may be, I might have gone to hell if it had not been for your reproofs and corrections."

Some of her neighbors, coming to visit her, asked her if she would leave them. She answered, "If you serve the Lord, you shall come to me in glory."

A little before she died, she had a great conflict with Satan and cried out, "I am none of his." Her mother, seeing her in trouble, asked her what was the matter. She answered, "Satan troubled me, but now I thank God all is well. I know I am none of his, but Christ's."

After this, she had a sense of God's love and a glorious sight as if she had seen the very heavens open, and the angels come to receive her, by which her heart was filled with joy and her tongue with praise.

Being desired by the bystanders to give them a particular account of what she saw, she answered, "You shall know hereafter." And so, in an ecstasy of joy and holy triumph, she went to heaven when she was about 12 years old. Hallelujah!

Example 4

*Of a child who began to look towards heaven
when she was about four years old, with some
observable passages in her life and at her death.*

A certain little child, when she was about four years
old, had a conscientious sense of her duty towards her
parents because the commandment said, "Honor thy
father and thy mother." And, though she had little
advantage of education, she carried it with the greatest
reverence to her parents imaginable, so that she was
no small credit as well as a comfort to them.

It was a usual thing for her to weep if she saw her
parents troubled, though she herself had not been the
occasion of it.

When she came from school, she would with grief
and abhorrence say that other children had sinned
against God by speaking grievous words which were so
bad that she dare not speak them again.

She would oftentimes be admitting of God's mercy
for such goodness to her rather than to others; that
she saw some begging, others blind, some deformed,
and that she lacked nothing that was good for her.

She was, many times and often, in one place or another in tears upon her knees.

This poor little thing would be ready to counsel
other little children how they ought to serve God,
putting them upon getting by themselves to pray. She
has been known, when her friends have been abroad,

Example 4   21

to teach children to pray, especially upon the Lord's
Day.

She very seriously begged the prayers of others that
they would remember her and that the Lord would
give her grace.

When this child saw some who were laughing,
whom she judged to be very wicked, she told them that
she feared that they had little reason to be merry. They
asked whether one might not laugh. She answered,
"No, indeed, until you have grace. They who are
wicked have more need to cry than to laugh."

She would say that it was the duty of parents,
masters, and mistresses, to reprove those under their
charge for sin, or else God will meet with them.

She would be very attentive when she read the
Scriptures, and be much affected with them.

She would by no means be persuaded to profane
the Lord's Day but would spend it in some good
duties.

When she went to school, it was willingly and
joyfully. She was very teachable and exemplary to other
children.

When she was taken sick, one asked her whether
she was willing to die. She answered, "Yes, if God would
pardon my sins." Being asked how her sins should be
pardoned, she answered, "Through the blood of
Christ."

She said she believed in Christ and desired and
longed to be with Him, and with a great deal of
cheerfulness gave up her soul to Him.

There were many observable passages in the life
and death of this child, but the hurry and grief that
her friends were in buried them.

Example 5

---

*Of the pious life and joyful death of a child who
died when he was about 12 years old.*

Charles Bridgman had no sooner learned to speak
than he took himself to pray.

He was very prone to learn the things of God.

He would sometimes be teaching them their duty
who waited upon him.

He learned by heart many good things before he
was well fit to go to school. And when he was sent to
school, he carried it so that all who observed him
either did or might admire him. O the sweet nature,
the good disposition, the sincere religion, which was in
him!

When he was at school, what was it that he desired
to learn but Christ and Him crucified?

So religious and exemplary were his words, his
actions so upright, his devotion so hearty, his fear of
God so great, that many were ready to say, as they did
of John, "What manner of child shall this be?"

He would be much in reading the Holy Scriptures.

He was desirous of more spiritual knowledge, and
would often be asking very serious and admirable
questions.

He would not stir out of doors before he had
poured out his soul to the Lord.

When he ate anything, he would be sure to lift up
his heart unto the Lord for a blessing upon it. And

Example 5   23

when he had moderately refreshed himself by eating, he would not forget to acknowledge God's goodness in feeding him.

He would not lie down in his bed until he had been on his knees. And sometimes, when he had forgotten his duty, he would quickly get out of his bed, kneel down upon his bare knees, and ask God's forgiveness for that sin.

He would rebuke his brethren if they were at any time too hasty at their meals and ate without asking a blessing. His check was usually this, "Dare you do this? God be merciful to us, this bit of bread might choke us!"

His sentences were wise and weighty, and might well have becomed some ancient Christian.

His sickness was a lingering disease, against which, to comfort him, one told him of possessions that must fall to his portion. "And what are they?" he said. "I would rather have the kingdom of heaven than a thousand such inheritances."

When he was sick, he seemed much taken up with heaven and asked very serious questions about the nature of his soul.

After he was pretty well satisfied about that, he inquired how his soul might be saved. The answer being made, "by the applying of Christ's merits by faith," he was pleased with the answer, and was ready to give any one who should desire it an account of his hope.

Being asked whether he would rather live or die, he answered, "I desire to die that I may go to my Savior."

His pains increased upon him, and one asked him whether he would rather still endure those pains or

forsake Christ. "Alas," said he, "I do not know what to
say, being a child, for these pains may stagger a strong
man, but I will strive to endure the best that I can."
Upon this, he called to mind that martyr, Thomas
Bilney,[1] who, being in prison the night before his
burning, put his finger into the candle to know how he
could endure the fire. "O," said the child, "had I lived
then, I would have run through the fire to have gone
to Christ!"

His sickness lasted long, and at least three days
before his death, he prophesied his departure, and not
only that he must die but the very day. "On the Lord's
Day," he said, "look to me." Neither was this a word of
course which you may guess by his often repetition,
every day asking until the day came indeed, "What, has
Sunday come?"

At last, the looked-for day came on, and no sooner
had the sun beautified the morning with its light but
he fell into a trance. His eyes were fixed, his face
cheerful, his lips smiled, his hands and face clasped in
a bow, as if he would have received some blessed angel
who was at hand to receive his soul. But he came to
himself and told them how he saw the sweetest body
that ever eyes beheld, who bid him to be of good
cheer, for he must presently go with him.

One who stood near him, now suspecting the time
of his dissolution nigh, bid him say, "Lord, into Thy
hands I commend my spirit, which is Thy due. Why?
For Thou hast redeemed it, O Lord, my God most

---

[1] Thomas Bilney (c.1495-1531), was a reform-minded Roman Catholic
martyr during the reign of Henry VIII of England. His life is described
in John Foxe's Book of Martyrs.

Example 5   25

true."
    The last words he spoke were exactly these, "Pray, pray, pray, nay, yet pray. And the more prayers, the better all prospers. God is the best Physician. Into Thy hands I commend my spirit. O Lord Jesus, receive my soul! Now I close my eyes. Forgive me, father, mother, brother, sister, all the world. Now I am well, my pain is almost gone, my joy is at hand. Lord, have mercy on me. O Lord, receive my soul unto Thee!"
    And thus he yielded his spirit up unto the Lord when he was about 12 years old.

Example 6

*Of a poor child who was awakened when
he was about five years old.*

A certain poor child, who had a very bad father, but, it was to be hoped, a very good mother, was, by the providence of God, brought to the sight of a godly friend of mine who, upon the first sight of the child, had a great pity for him and took an affection to him, with a mind to bring him up for Christ.

At first, with great sweetness and kindness, he allured the child, by which means it was not long before he got a deep interest in the heart of the child, and he began to obey him with more readiness than children usually do their parents.

By this, a door was opened for a farther work. An. He had a greater advantage to instill spiritual principles into the soul of the child, which he was not lacking in, as the Lord gave opportunity and the child was capable.

It was not long before the Lord was pleased to strike in with the spiritual exhortations of this good man, so that the child was brought to a liking of the things of God.

He quickly learned a great part of the Assembly's catechism by heart, and that before he could even read his primer. And he took a great delight in learning his catechism.

He was not only able to give a very good account of

Example 6   27

his catechism but would answer such questions as are not in the catechism with greater understanding than could be expected from one of his age.

He took great delight in discoursing about the things of God. And when my friend had either been praying or reading, expounding or repeating sermons, he seemed very attentive and ready to receive the truth of God. He would, with incredible gravity, diligence and affection, wait until duties were ended, to the no-small joy and admiration of those who observed him.

He would ask very excellent questions and discourse about the condition of his soul and heavenly things. He seemed mightily concerned what should become of his soul when he should die, so that his discourse made some Christians even to stand astonished.

He was greatly taken with the great kindness of Christ in dying for sinners, and would be in tears at the mention of them, and seemed at a strange rate to be affected with the unspeakable love of Christ.

When nobody had been speaking to him, he would burst out into tears and, being asked the reason, he would say that the very thought of Christ's love to sinners in suffering for them made him so that he could not help but cry.

Before he was six years old, he made conscience of secret prayer. And when he prayed, it was with such extraordinary melting that his eyes have looked red and sore with weeping by himself for his sins.

He would be putting Christians upon spiritual discourse when he saw them, and seemed little satisfied unless they were talking of good things.

It is evident that this poor child's thoughts were very much busied about the things of another world, for he would oftentimes be speaking to his bedfellow at midnight about the matters of his soul. And when he could not sleep he would take heavenly conference to be sweeter than his appointed rest. This was his usual custom, and thus he would provoke and put forward an experienced Christian to spend waking hours in talking of God and the everlasting rest.

Not long after this, his good mother died, which went very near his heart, for he greatly honored his mother.

After the death of his mother, he would often repeat some of the promises that are made unto fatherless children, especially that in Exodus 22:22, "Ye shall not afflict any widow, or fatherless child; if thou afflict them in any wise, and they cry at all unto Me, I will surely hear their cry." These words he would often repeat with tears and say, "I am fatherless and motherless upon earth; yet, if any wrongs me, I have a Father in heaven who will take my part. To Him I commit myself, and in Him is all my trust."

Thus he continued in a course of holy duties, living in the fear of God. He showed wonderful grace for a child and died sweetly in the faith of Jesus.

My friend, from whom I received this information, is a judicious Christian of many years' experience, who was no ways related to him, but was a constant eye and ear witness of his godly life, and his honorable and cheerful death.

Example 7

Of a notoriously wicked child who was taken up from begging and admirably converted; with an account of his holy life and joyful death when he was nine years old.

A very poor child of the parish of Newington-Butts came begging to the door of a dear Christian friend of mine in a most lamentable condition. But it pleased God to raise in the heart of my friend a great pity and tenderness towards this poor child, so that in charity he took him out of the streets whose parents were unknown and who had nothing at all in him to commend him to anyone's charity but his misery. My friend, eyeing the glory of God and the good of the immortal soul of this wretched creature, discharged the parish of the child and took him as his own, designing to bring him up in the fear of the Lord. A noble piece of charity! And that which made the kindness far greater was that there seemed to be very little hope of doing any good for this child, for he was a very monster of wickedness and a thousand times more miserable and vile by his sin than by his poverty.

He was running to hell as fast as he could go. He was old in naughtiness when he was young in years. And one shall scarcely hear of one so like the devil in his infancy as this poor child was. What sin was there (that his age was capable of) that he did not commit? By the corruption of his nature and the abominable example of little beggar-boys, he had arrived to a strange pitch of impiety. He would call filthy names, take God's name in vain, curse and swear, and do almost all kind of mischief. As to anything of God, he was worse than a heathen.

But this sin and misery was but a stronger motive to that gracious man to pity him and to do all that he possibly could to pluck this fire-brand out of the fire. And it was not long before the Lord was pleased to let him understand that He had a design of everlasting kindness upon the soul of this poor child. For no sooner had this good man taken this creature into his house but he prayed for him, and labored with all his might to convince him of his miserable condition by nature and to teach him something of God, the worth of his soul, and that eternity of glory or misery that he was born to. Blessed be free grace, it was not long before the Lord was pleased to show him that it was He who put into his heart to take in this child that he might bring him up for Christ.

The Lord soon struck in with his godly instructions, so that an amazing change was seen in the child. In a few weeks space, he was soon convinced of the evil of his ways. Now there was no more news of his calling names, swearing or cursing. No more taking the Lord's name in vain. He became civil and respectable, and such a strange alteration was wrought in the child that all the parish that rung of his villainy before was now ready to talk of his reformation. His company, his talk, his employment were all changed, and he was like another creature, so that the glory of God's free grace began already to shine in him.

And this change was not only an external one, and thus discerned abroad, but he would get by himself

Example 7   31

and weep and mourn bitterly for his horribly wicked life, as might easily be perceived by those who lived in the house with him.

It was the great care of his godly master to strike in with those convictions which the Lord had made, and to improve them as he could. And he was not a little glad to see his labor was not in vain in the Lord. He still experienced that the Lord carries on His own work mightily upon the heart of the child. He was still more and more broken under a sense of his undone state by nature. He was often in tears, bemoaning his lost and miserable condition. When his master spoke earnestly of the things of God, he listened earnestly, and took in with much delight and affection what he was taught. Seldom was there any discourse about soul matters in his hearing but he heard it as if it were for his life, and would weep greatly.

He would, after his master had been speaking to him or others about the things of God, go to him and question him about them, begging him to instruct and teach him further and to tell him those things again that he might better remember and understand them.

Thus he continued seeking after the knowledge of God in Christ and practicing holy duties until the sickness with which the child was smitten came into the house. At first, the poor child was greatly amazed and afraid. And though his pains were great and his distemper very tedious, yet the sense of his sin and the thought of the miserable condition that he feared his soul was still in made his trouble ten times greater. He was in grievous agonies of spirit, and his former sins stared him in the face and made him tremble. The poison of God's arrows drank up his spirit. The sense of sin and wrath was so great that he could not tell what in the world to do. The weight of God's displeasure and the thoughts of lying under it to all eternity broke him to pieces. He cried out very bitterly, "What shall I do?" He was a miserable sinner, and he feared that he should go to hell. His sins had been so great and so many that there were no hopes for him. He was not by far so much concerned for his life as for his soul, what would become of that forever. Now the plague upon his body seemed nothing to that which was in his soul.

But in this great distress, the Lord was pleased to send one to take care of his soul, who urged upon him the great and precious promises which were made to one in his condition, telling him that there was enough in Christ for the chief of sinners and that He came to seek and to save such a poor lost creature as he was. But this poor child found it a very difficult thing for him to believe that there was any mercy for such a dreadful sinner as he had been.

He was made to cry out of himself not only for his swearing, lying, and other outwardly notorious sins, but he was in great horror for the sin of his nature, for the vileness of his heart, and for original corruption under it. He was in so great anguish that the trouble of his spirit made him, in a great measure, to forget the pains of his body.

He particulary confessed and bewailed his sins with tears, and some sins so secret that none in the world could charge him with.

He would condemn himself for sin as deserving to have no mercy, and thought that there was not a greater sinner in all of London than himself. He

Example 7   33

abhorred himself as the vilest creature he knew.

He not only prayed much with strong cries and tears himself, but he begged the prayers of Christians for him.

He would ask Christians whether they thought there was any hope for him, and would beg them to deal plainly with him, for he was greatly afraid of being deceived.

Being informed how willing and ready the Lord Jesus was to accept poor sinners upon their repentance and turning, and being counselled to venture himself upon Christ for mercy and salvation, he said he would cast himself upon Christ. But he could not but wonder how Christ should be willing to die for such a vile wretch as he was. And he found it one of the hardest things in the world to believe.

But at last it pleased the Lord to give him some small hopes that there might be mercy for him, for he had been the chief of sinners. And he was made to lay a little hold upon such promises as this, "Come unto Me, all ye that are weary and heavy laden, and I will give you rest." But O how this poor boy admired and blessed God for the least hopes! How highly he advanced free and rich grace that should pity and pardon him! And at last he was full of praise and admiring God, so that (to speak in the words of a good man who was an eye and an ear witness) to the praise and glory of God let it be spoken, the house at that day, for all the sickness in it, was a little lower heaven, so full of joy and praise was it.

The child grew exceedingly in knowledge, experience, patience, humility, and self-abhorrence. And he thought he could never speak badly enough of himself.

The name that he would call himself by was "a toad."

And, though he prayed before, yet now the Lord poured out upon him the spirit of prayer in an extraordinary manner for one of his age. So that now he prayed more frequently, more earnestly, more spiritually than ever. O how eagerly would he beg to be washed in the blood of Jesus! And that the King of Kings and Lord of Lords over heaven, earth, and sea, would pardon and forgive him all his sins and receive his soul into His kingdom. And what he spoke was with so much life and fervor of spirit that it filled the hearers with astonishment and joy.

He had no small sense of the use and excellency of Christ and such longings and breathings of his soul after Him that, when mention had been made of Christ, he was ready almost to leap out of his bed for joy.

He was told that, if he should recover, he must not live as he pleased but he must give himself up to Christ and be His child and servant, bear His yoke and be obedient to His laws, live a holy life and take His cross, and suffer mocking, and reproach and (it may be) persecution for His name's sake. "Now, child," said one to him, "are you willing to have Christ upon such terms?" He signified his willingness by the earnestness of his looks and words and the casting up of his eyes to heaven, saying, "Yes, with all my soul, the Lord helping me, I will do this."

Yet he had many doubts and fears and was ever and always harping upon this or that. Though he was willing, yet Christ, he feared, was not willing to accept him because of the greatness of his sins. Yet his hopes were greater than his fears.

The Wednesday before he died, the child lay, as it

Example 7   35

were, in a trance for about half an hour, in which time
he thought he saw a vision of angels. When he was out
of his trance, he was a little uneasy and asked his nurse
why she did not let him go. "Go where, child?" said
she. "Why, along with those brave gentlemen," said he.
"But they told me they would come and fetch me away
from all you on next Friday." And he doubled his
words many times, "Upon next Friday, those brave gentlemen will come for me." And upon that day, the
child died joyfully.

He was very thankful to his master, and very sensible of his great kindness in taking him up out of the
streets when he was begging, and he admired the
goodness of God, which put it into the mind of a
stranger to look upon, and to take such fatherly care of
such a pitiful, sorry creature as he was. "O my dear
master," he said, "I hope to see you in heaven, for I am
sure you will go there. O blessed be the God that made
you to take pity upon me, for I might have died and
gone to the devil and have been damned forever, if it
had not been for you."

The Thursday before he died, he asked a very godly
friend of mine what he thought of his condition, and
where his soul was going. For he said he could not still
but fear lest he should deceive himself with false
hopes.

At this point my friend spoke to him thus, "Child,
for all that I have endeavored to hold forth the grace
of God in Christ to your soul, and given you a warrant
from the Word of God that Christ is as freely offered to
you as to any sinner in the world; if you are willing to
accept Him, you may have Christ, and all that you
want, with Him. And yet, you give way to these doubt-

ings and fears as though I told you nothing but lies. You say you fear that Christ will not accept you. I fear that you are not heartily willing to accept Him!"

The child answered, "Indeed, I am."

"Why, then, child, if you are sincerely willing to have Christ, I tell you, He is a thousand times more willing to have you and wash you and save you than you are to desire it. And now, at this time, Christ offers Himself freely to you again. Therefore, receive Him humbly by faith into your heart, and bid Him welcome, for He deserves it."

Upon these words, the Lord revealed His love to the child. And he gave a kind of leap in his bed and snapped his fingers and thumb together with an abundance of joy, as much as to say, "Well, yes, all is well. The match is made. Christ is willing and I am willing too. And now Christ is mine and I am His forever."

And from that time forward, in full joy and assurance of God's love, he continued earnestly praising God, with desiring to die and be with Christ. And on Friday morning, he sweetly went to rest, using that very expression, "Into Thy hands, I commit my spirit." He died punctually at that time of which he had spoken, and in which he expected those angels to come to him. He was not much above nine years old when he died.

This narrative I had from a judicious, holy man, unrelated to him, who was an eye and ear witness to all these things.

THE END OF THE FIRST PART

A Token
for Children

Preface

Christian Reader,

In the former part of my *Token for Children,* I promised, in part, that if that piece met with kind entertainment, it might be followed with a second of the same nature. If it did not seem a little to savor of vanity, I might tell the world what encouragement I have met with in this work. But this I will only say: I have met with so much as has made me give this little book leave to go abroad into the world. I am not ignorant as to what discouragement I may meet with from some, but as long as I am sure I shall not meet with this, that it is improbable if not impossible that it should save a soul. I think the rest may easily be answered or warrantably slighted. But because I am persuaded by some that one example in the former (that of a child who began to be serious between two

37

and three years old) was scarcely credible, and they feared might prejudice the authority of the rest, I shall say something to answer that.

Those who make this objection are either good or bad. If they are bad, I expect never to satisfy them, unless I tell them of a romance or play, or something that might suit a carnal mind. It is like holiness in older persons, it is a matter of contempt and scorn to them, much more in such as these I mention. The truth of it is, it is no wonder at all to me that the subjects of Satan should not be very pleased with that whose design is to undermine the interest of their great master. Nothing will satisfy some unless Christ and holiness may be degraded and vilified. But hold, sinner, hold; never hope it. Heaven shall never be turned into hell for your sake. And as for all your atheistic objections, scoffs, and jeers, they shall before long be fully answered, and the hosannas and hallelujahs of these babes shall condemn your oaths, blasphemies, and jeers. Then you will be silenced. And unless converting grace turns your heart quickly, you will forever rue your madness and folly when it is too late to remedy it.

But if the persons who make this objection are godly, I do not question but that I may give them reasonable satisfaction.

First, consider who it was that I had that example from. It was Mrs. Jeofries, in Long Lane, in Mary Magdalen Bermondsey Parish, in the County of Surry, a woman of that fame in the Church of Christ for her exemplary piety, wisdom, experience, and singular watchfulness over every small detail that she speaks. I do not question but that her name is precious to most of the ministers of London, at least in Borough. And, as a reverend divine said, "She is such a mother in Israel that her single testimony is of as much authority almost as any single ministers."

Having since discoursed this matter with her, she calls God to witness that she has spoken nothing but the truth. She failed only in this: She did not speak by far as much as she might have done concerning that sweet babe. I might add that I have since seen a godly gentleman out of the country who professed to me that he had seen as much as that in a little one of the same age, who since that time, I hear, went sweetly to heaven.

Does not the Reverend Mr. [Samuel] Clarke[1] in his works quote a child of two years old who looked towards heaven? Does not credible history acquaint us with a martyr of seven years old, who was whippled almost to death and never shed one tear, nor complained, and, at last, had his head struck off?

I do not speak of these as common matters, but record them among those stupendous acts of Him who can as easily work wonders as not. What is too hard for the Almighty? Has God said He will work no more wonders? I think most of God's work in the business of conversion call for admiration. And I believe that silence, or rather praise, would better become saints than questioning the truth of such things, especially

---

[1] This is probably a reference to one of the works of Samuel Clarke (1599-1683), perhaps his English Martyrologie first published in 1652. Clarke was a Puritan preacher and writer who, after his ejection from the Church of England ministry in 1662, devoted himself largely to writing, especially biographies. Clarke was a friend of Richard Baxter, and officiated at Baxter's wedding ceremony.

where an apparent injury is thereby done to the
interest of Christ, the honor of God's grace, and the
reputation of so eminent a saint.

I judge this sufficient to satisfy most. As for others, I
do not trouble myself. If I may but promote the
interest of Christ and the good of souls, and give up
my account with joy, it is enough.

That the Lord would bless my endeavors to these
ends, I beg the prayers of all saints, and yours also,
sweet children who fear the Lord. And that all parents
and masters would assist me with their warm application of these things, and that children may be their
crown and their joy, is the prayer of one who desires to
love Christ and little children dearly.

James Janeway

Example 8

*Of a child who was very serious at four years old,
with an account of his comfortable death when
he was 12 years and three weeks old.*

John Sudlow was born of religious parents in the
county of Middlesex, whose great care was to instill
spiritual principles into him as soon as he was capable
of understanding them, and whose endeavors the Lord
was pleased to crown with success. To use the expression of a holy man concerning him, scarcely more
could be expected or desired from one so little.

When he was scarcely able to speak plainly, he
seemed to have a very great awe and reverence of God
upon his spirit and a strange sense of the things of another world, as might easily be perceived by those serious and admirable questions which he would often be
asking of those Christians with whom he thought he
might be bold.

The first thing that most affected him and made
him endeavor to escape from the wrath to come, and
to inquire what he should do to be saved, was the
death of a little brother. When he saw him without
breath, and unable to speak or stir, and when he was
carried out of doors and put into a pit hole, he was
greatly concerned and asked surprising questions
about him. But that which most affected him and others was whether he must die too. This being answered,
it made such a deep impression upon him that from

41

that time forward he was exceedingly serious. This was
when he was about four years old.

Now he was desirous to know what he might do that
he might live in another world, and what he must
avoid that he might not die forever. Being instructed
by his godly parents, he soon labored to avoid whatever
might displease God. Now, if you told him that anything was sinful, and that God would not have him to
do it, he was easily kept from it. And, even at this time
of day, the apprehensions of God, death, and eternity
laid such a restrait upon him that he would not, for a
world, have told a lie.

He quickly learned to read exactly, and took such
pleasure in reading the Scriptures and his catechism
and other good books that it is scarcely to be paralleled. He would naturally run to his book without bid-
ding when he came home from school. When other
children of his age and acquaintance were playing, he
reckoned it his recreation to be doing that which is
good.

When he was older, he would ask his maid serious
questions, and pray her to teach him his catechism or
Scriptures or some other good thing. He took no
delight in common discourse but most eagerly desired
to be sucking in the knowledge of the things of God,
Christ, his soul, and another world.

He was greatly taken with reading Foxe's *Book of
Martyrs*,[1] and would be ready to leave his dinner to go

---

[1] *The Book of Martyrs* was an abridgement of John Foxe's *Acts and
Monuments*, first published in 1563. John Foxe (1516-1587) wrote the
book especially to commemorate Protestants who died beneath Roman
Catholic persecution, although it began with first century martyrs. At

Example 8   43

to his book.

He was exceedingly careful of redeeming and improving time. Scarcely a moment of it, but he would give an excellent account of the experience of it, so that this child might have taught elder persons—and would doubtless have condemned their idle and unaccountable wastings of those precious hours in which they should, as this sweet child, have been laying in provision for eternity.

He could not endure to read anything over slightly, but whatever he read he dwelt upon, laboring to understand it thoroughly and remember it. And whatever he could not understand, he would often ask his father or mother the meaning of it.

When any Christian friends had been discoursing with his father, if they began to talk anything about religion, to be sure they should have his company. Of his own accord he would leave all to hear anything of Christ. And he would creep as close to them as he could, and listen as affectionately, though it was only for an hour or two. He was scarcely ever known to express the least token of weariness while he was hearing anything that was good. And sometimes, when neighbor's children came and called out to him to entice him, and begged him to go with them, he could by no means be persuaded—though he might have had permission from his parents—if he had any hopes that any good friend would come into his father's house.

He was very modest while any stranger was present, and was loath to ask them any questions. But as soon as

---

one time, Foxe's Book of Martyrs was the most read book in English next to the Bible.

they were gone, he would let his father know that there
was little said or done but he observed it, and would
reflect upon what had passed in their discourses, and
desire satisfaction in what he could not understand at
present.

He was a boy of prodigious intellect and maturity
for his age, as will appear from his solid and rational
questions. I shall mention but two of many.

The first was this. When he was reading by himself
in [Michael] Drayton's poems[2] about Noah's flood and
the ark, he asked who built the ark. The answer came
that it was likely that Noah hired men to help him
build it. Would they, he said, build an ark to save
another, and not go into it themselves?

Another question he put was this: who has a greater
glory, saints or angels? The answer which came was
that angels were the most excellent of creatures, and it
is to be thought their nature is made capable of
greater glory than man's. He said that he was of another mind, and his reason was because angels were
servants while saints are children, and that Christ never
took upon Himself the nature of angels but the nature
of saints. By being man, He advanced human nature
above the nature of angels.

By this you may perceive the greatness of his
maturity and the bent of his thoughts. Thus he
continued for several years together, laboring to get
more and more spiritual knowledge and to prepare for

---

[2] Michael Drayton (1563-1631) wrote mostly secular poetry, but
published his The Muses Elizium lately discovered by a new way over
Parnassus in 1630, which contained some poems on Old Testament
themes.

Example 8   45

an endless life.

He was a child of an excellent, sweet temper, wonderfully dutiful to his parents, ready and joyful to do what he was bid, and by no means would he do anything to displease them. If they were at anytime angry, he would not stir from them until they were thoroughly reconciled to him.

He was not only good himself, but would do what he could to make others so too—especially those who were nearest to him. He was very watchful over his brothers and sisters, and would not suffer them to use any unhandsome words or do any unhandsome action. But he would be putting them upon that which was good. And when at any time he rebuked them, it was not childishly and slightly but with that great gravity and seriousness, as one who was not a little concerned for God's honor and the eternal welfare of their souls.

He would go to his father and mother with great tenderness and compassion (being far from telling of tales), and beg them to take more care of the souls of his brothers and sisters. He urged them to take heed lest they should go on in a sinful and Christless state and prove their sorrow and shame, and go to hell when they die and be ruined forever.

He was exceedingly affected with hearing the Word of God preached. He could not be satisfied unless he could carry home much of the substance of what he heard. To this end, he quickly got to learn shorthand, and would give a very fine account of any sermon that he heard.

He was much engaged in secret prayer and reading the Scriptures. To be sure, morning and evening he would be by himself and was, no question, wrestling with God.

He would get choice Scriptures by heart, and was perfect at his catechism.

The providences of God were not passed by without considerable observation by him.

In the time of the plague, he was exceedingly concerned about his soul and everlasting state, very much by himself upon his knees. This prayer was found written in shorthand after his death:

> O Lord God and merciful Father, take pity upon me, a miserable sinner, and strengthen me, O Lord, in Thy faith, and make me one of Thy glorious saints in heaven. O Lord, keep me from this poisonous infection. However, not my will but Thy will be done, O Lord, on earth as it is in heaven. But, O Lord, if Thou hast appointed me to die by it, O Lord, fit me for death and give me a good heart to bear up under my afflictions! O Lord God and merciful Father, take pity on me, Thy poor child. Teach me, O Lord, Thy Word. Make me strong in faith. O Lord, I have sinned against Thee. Lord, pardon my sins. I would have been in hell long ago if it had not been for Thy mercy. O Lord, I pray Thee to keep my parents in the truth and save them from this affliction, if it be Thy will, that they may live to bring me up in the truth. O Lord, I pray Thee, stay this infection that rages in this city, and pardon their sins, and try them once more, and see if they will turn to Thee. Save me, O Lord, from this infection that I may live to praise and glorify Thy name. But, O Lord, if Thou hast appointed me to die of it, fit me for death that I may die with comfort; and, O Lord, I pray Thee to help me to bear up under all afflictions for Christ's sake. Amen.

Example 8   47

He was not a little concerned for the whole nation, and begged that God would pardon the sins of this land and bring it nearer himself.

About the beginning of November 1665, this sweet child was smitten with the distemper, but he carried it with admirable patience under the hand of God.

These are some of his dying expressions:

"The Lord shall be my Physician, for He will cure both soul and body."

"Heaven is the best hospital."

"It is the Lord, let Him do what seemeth good in His eyes."

"It is the Lord that takes away my health, but I will says as Job did, 'Blessed be the name of the Lord.'"

"If I should live longer, I shall but sin against God."

Looking upon his father, he said, "If the Lord would but lend me the least finger of His hand to lead me through the dark entry of death, I will rejoice in Him."

When a minister came to him, among other things he spoke concerning life. He said, "This is a wicked world, yet it is good to live with my parents, but it is better to live in heaven."

An hour and a half before his death, the same minister came again to visit him and asked him, "Are you not afraid to die?"

He answered, "No, if the Lord will but comfort me in that hour."

"But," said the minister, "how can you expect comfort, seeing we deserve none?"

He answered, "No, if I had my deserts, I would have been in hell long ago."

"But," replied the minister, "which way do you expect comfort and salvation, seeing you are a sinner?"

He answered, "In Christ alone." In whom, about an hour and a half after, he fell asleep, saying he would take a long sleep, and charging them who were around him not to wake him.

He died when he was twelve years, three weeks, and a day old.

Example 9

*Of a child who was very eminent when she was
between five and six years old, with some
memorable passages of her life.*

Ann Lane was born at Colebrook in the county of
Bucks. She was no sooner able to speak plainly and
express any thing considerable of reason than she began to act as if she was sanctified from the very womb.

She was very solicitous about her soul—what would
become of it when she should die, where she should
live forever, and what she should do to be saved—
when she was about five years old.

She was inclined to be often engaged in secret
prayer and in pouring out her soul in such a manner
as is rarely to be heard of from one of her years.

I, having occasion to lodge at Colebrook, sent for
her father, an old disciple, an Israelite indeed. I desired him to give me some account of his experiences,
and how the Lord first was wrought upon him.

He gave me this answer. He was, from a child,
somewhat civil, honest, and harmless, but was little acquainted with the power of religion until this sweet
child put him upon a thorough inquiry into the state
of his soul. She would still be begging and pleading
with him to redeem his time, to act with life and vigor
in the things of God, which was no small demonstra-
tion to him of the reality of invisible things. She was
greatly concerned not only about her own soul but

about her father's too, which was the occasion of his conversion. The very thought of it was a quickening of him for 30 years, and he hoped never to wear off the impressions of it from his spirit.

After this, she (as I remember) put her father upon family duties. If at any time he was long absent from his shop, she would find him out and with much sweetness and humility beg him to come home and remember the preciousness of time for which we must all given an account.

She was grieved if she saw any who conversed with her father if they were unprofitable, unsavory, or long in their discourse of common things.

Her own language was the language of Canaan. How solidly, profitably, and spiritually she would talk! She made good people take great delight in her company, and justly drew the admiration of all that she knew.

She could not endure the company of common children, nor play, but was quite above all those things which most children are taken with. Her business was to be reading, praying, discoursing about the things of God, and any kind of business that her age and strength were capable of. She would not be idle by any means.

It was the greatest recreation to her to hear any good people talking about God, Christ, their souls, the Scriptures, or anything that concerned another life.

She had a strange contempt of the world, and scorned those things which most are much too pleased with. She could not be brought to wear any laces or anything she thought was superfluous.

She would complain to her parents if she saw

Example 9   51

anything in them that she judged would not be for the honor of religion or suitable to that condition which the providence of God had set them in the world.

The child was the joy and delight of all the Christians thereabout in those times. And she was still quickening and raising the spirits of those who talked with her. This poor babe was a great help to both father and mother, and her memory is sweet to this day.

She continued thus to walk as a stranger in the world, as one who was making haste to a better place. And, after she had done a great deal of work for God, and her own soul and the souls of others too, she was called home to rest and was received into the arms of Jesus before she was 10 years old.

Example 10

Of a child who was awakened when she was between
seven and eight years old, with some account of
her last hours and triumphant death.

Tabitha Adler was the daughter of a holy and reverend minister in Kent who lived near Gravesend. She was much instructed in the Holy Scriptures and her catechism by her father and mother, but there appeared nothing extraordinary in her until she was between seven and eight years old.

About which time, when she was sick, one asked her what she thought would become of her if she should die. She answered that she was greatly afraid that she should go to hell.

Being asked why she was afraid of going to hell, she answered that it was because she feared she did not love God.

Again, being asked how she knew that she did not love God, she replied, "What have I done for God since I was born? And besides this, I have been taught that he who loves God keeps His commandments; but I have kept none of them at all!"

Being further demanded if she would not gladly love God she answered, "Yes, with all my heart, if I could, but I find it a hard thing to love One I do not see."

She was advised to beg God for a heart to love Him. She answered, "I am afraid it is too late."

Example 10   53

Being asked again whether she was not sorry that she could not love God, she answered, "Yes, but I am still afraid it is too late."

Seeing her in such a desponding condition, a dear friend of hers spent the next day in fasting and prayer for her.

After this, that Christian friend asked her how she was doing now. She answered with a great deal of joy that now she blessed the Lord. She loved the Lord Jesus dearly, and felt that she loved Him. "Oh," said she, "I love Him dearly!"

"Why," said her friend, "did you not say yesterday that you did not love the Lord and that you could not? What did you mean to speak so strangely?"

"Surely," said she, "it was Satan that put it into my mind; but now I love Him. O blessed be God for the Lord Jesus Christ."

After this, she had a discovery of her approaching death, which was no small comfort to her. "Soon," she said with a holy triumph, "I shall be with Jesus. I am married to Him. He is my Husband and I am His bride. I have given myself to Him and He has given Himself to me, and I shall live with Him forever."

This strange language made the hearers stand astonished. But thus she continued for some little time in a kind of ecstasy of joy, admiring the excellency of Christ, rejoicing in her interest in Him, and longing to be with Him.

After awhile, some of her friends, standing by her, observed a more than ordinary earnestness and fixedness in her countenance. They said one to another, "Look how earnestly she looks. Surely she sees something."

One asked what it was she fixed her eyes upon so eagerly. One who was nearby said, "I warrant that she sees death coming."

"No," she said, "it is glory that I see. It is what I fix my eyes upon."

One asked her what glory was like. She answered, "I can't speak what, but I am going to it. Will you go with me? I am going to glory. O that all of you were to go with me to that glory!"

With these words, her soul took wing and went to the possession of the glory that she had some believing sight of before. She died when she was between eight and nine years old.

Example 11

Of a child who was greatly affected with the things of God when she was very young, with an exact account of her admirable behavior upon her deathbed.

Susannah Bicks was born at Leyden, in Holland, January 24, 1650, of very religious parents, whose great care was to instruct and catechize their child and to present her to the ministers of the place to be publicly instructed and catechized.

It pleased the Lord to bless the holy education and good example of her parents, and their catechizing, to the good of her soul, so that she soon had a true savor and relish of what she was taught and made an admirable use of it in a time of need, as you shall hear afterwards.

She was a child of great dutifulness to her parents, and of a very sweet, humble, spiritual nature. And not only the truth but the power and eminency of religion shone in her so clearly that she not only comforted the hearts of her parents but drew the admiration of all who were witnesses of God's works of love upon her. She may well be proposed as a pattern not only to children but to persons of riper years.

She continued in a course of religious duties for some considerable time so that her life was more excellent than most Christians, but in her last sickness she excelled herself. Her deportment was so admirable that, partly through wonder and astonishment and partly through sorrow, many observable things were passed by without committing to paper which deserved to have been written in letters of gold. But take these which follow as some of many which were taken from her dying lips and first published by religious and judicious Christians in Dutch, afterwards translated and, with a little alteration of the style (for the benefit of English children), brought into this form by me.

In the month of August 1664, when the pestilence raged so much in Holland, this sweet child was smitten. And as soon as she felt herself very ill, she was said to break forth with abundance of sense and feeling in these following words, "If Thy law were not my delight, I should perish in my affliction."

Her father, coming to her to encourage her in sickness, said to her, "Be of good comfort, my child, for the Lord will be near to you and us under this heavy and sore trial. He will not forsake us though He chastens us."

"Yea father," said she, "our heavenly Father chastens us for our profit, that we may be partakers of His holiness. 'No chastisement seemeth for the present to be joyous but grievous, but afterwards it yieldeth the peaceable fruit of righteousness to them which are exercised thereby.' The Lord is now chastening me upon this sick bed, but I hope He will bless it so to me as to cause it to yield to me that blessed fruit, according to the riches of His mercies which fail not."

After that, she spake to God with her eyes lifted up to heaven, saying, "Be merciful to me, O Father, be merciful to me a sinner, according to Thy word."

Then, looking upon her sorrowful parents, she said, "It is said, 'Cast thy burden upon the Lord and

Example 11   57

He shall sustain thee, and He will never suffer the righteous to be moved.' Therefore, my dear father and mother, cast all your care upon Him who causes all things to go well that concern you."

Her mother said unto her, "O my dear child, I have no small comfort from the Lord in you, and the fruit of His grace whereby you have been so much exercised unto godliness in reading the Word, in prayer and gracious discourse, to the edification of yourself and us. The Lord Himself, who gave you to us, make up this loss, if it be His pleasure to take you away from us."

"Dear mother," said she, "though I leave you, and you leave me, yet God will never leave us. For it is said, 'Can a woman forget her sucking child that she should not have compassion on the fruit of her womb, yet will not I forget thee; behold I have graven thee upon the palms of My hands.' Oh, comfortable words both for mother and children! Mark, dear mother, how fast the Lord keeps and holds His people, that He even graves them upon the palms of His hands. Though I must part with you, and you with me, yet, blessed be God, He will never part either from you or me."

Being weary with much speaking, she desired to rest awhile. But after a little time awaking again, her father asked her how it was with her. She made no direct answer but asked what day it was. Her father said it was the Lord's day.

"Well, then," said she," have you given up my name to be remembered in the public prayers of the church?" Her father told her he had.

"I have learned," said she, "that the effectual fervent prayer of the righteous avails much."

She had a very high esteem for the faithful ministers of Christ, and much desired their company where she was. But knowing the hazard that such a visit might expose them and the church to, she would by no means suffer that the minister should come near her person, but chose rather to throw herself upon the arms of the Lord and to improve that knowledge she had in the Word, her former experience and the visits of private Christians, and those which the church had appointed in such cases to visit and comfort the sick.

One of those who came to visit her was of very great use to her to comfort her and lift her up, in some measure, above the fears of death.

Though young, she was very much concerned for the interest of God and religion, for gospel ministers, and for the sins and the decay of the power of godliness in her own country which will further appear by what may follow.

Her father, coming in to her, found her in an extraordinary passion of weeping and asked her what was the cause of her great sorrow. She answered, "Have I not cause to weep when I hear that Mr. De Wit was taken sick this day in his pulpit and went home very ill. Is not this a sad sign of God's displeasure to our country, when God smites such a faithful pastor?"

She had a high valuation of God and would speak in David's language. "Whom have I in heaven but Thee, and there is none upon earth I can desire in comparison of Thee." She was much lifted up above the fears of death. What else was the meaning of such expressions as these? "How do I long! Even as the hart panteth after the water-brooks, so my soul panteth after Thee, O God, for God, the living God. When shall I come and appear before God?"

Example 11   59

She was a great hater of sin and, with much grief and self abhorrence, reflected upon it. But that which lay most upon her heart was the corruption of her nature and original sin. How often would she cry out in the words of the psalmist, "Behold I was shapen in iniquity, and in sin did my mother conceive me, and I was altogether born in sin." She could never lay herself low enough under a sense of that original sin which she brought with her into the world.

She spoke many things most judiciously of the old man and putting it off, and of the new man and putting it on; which showed that she was no stranger to conversion and that she, in some measure, understood what mortification, self-denial, and taking up of her cross and following Christ meant. That Scripture was much in her mouth, "The sacrifices of God are a contrite heart, a broken and a contrite Spirit O God, Thou wilt not despise." "That brokenness of heart," said she, "which is built upon and flows from faith, and that faith which is built upon Christ, who is the proper and only sacrifice for sin." These are her own words.

Afterwards, she desired to rest. When she had slumbered awhile she said, "Oh, dear father and mother, how weak do I feel myself!"

"My dear child," said her father, "God will, in His tender mercy, strengthen you in your weakness."

"Yea father," said she, "that is my confidence. For it is said, 'The bruised reed He will not break, and the smoking flax He will not quench.' "

Then she discoursed excellently of the nature of faith and desired that the 11th chapter of Hebrews should be read unto her, at the reading of which she cried out, "Oh, what a steadfast faith was that of

Abraham which made him willing to offer up his own and only son! 'Faith is the substance of the things hoped for, the evidence of things not seen.' "

Her father and mother, hearing her excellent discourse and seeing her admirable conduct, burst out into abundance of tears, upon which she pleaded with them to be patient and content with the hand of God. "Oh," said she, "why do you weep at this rate over me seeing, I hope, you have no reason to question but if the Lord takes me out of this miserable world, it shall be well with me to all eternity. You ought to be well satisfied, seeing it is said, 'God is in heaven and doth whatsoever pleaseth Him.' And do you not pray every day that the will of God may be done upon earth as it is in heaven? Now father, this is God's will that I should lie upon this sick bed of this disease: Shall we not be content when our prayers are answered? Would not your extreme sorrow be murmuring against God without whose good pleasure nothing comes to pass? Although I am struck with this sad disease, yet, it is the will of God that silences me and I will, as long as I live, pray that God's will be done, and not mine."

Seeing her parents still very much moved, she further argued with them from the providence of God which had a special hand in every common thing, much more in the disposal of the lives of men and women. "Are not two sparrows sold for a farthing, and not one of them falls to the ground without our heavenly Father? Yea, the hairs of our head are all numbered. 'Therefore, fear not. You are of more value than many sparrows.' Adversity and prosperity are both good. Some things seem evil in our eyes, but the Lord turns all to good for those who are His."

Example 11 61

She came then to speak particularly concerning the plague. "Does not," said she, "the pestilence come from God? Why else does the Scripture say, 'Shall there be evil in the city which I have not sent?' What do those people mean who say the pestilence comes from the air. Is not the Lord the creator and ruler of the air, and are not the elements under His government? Or, if they say it comes from the earth, has He not the same power and influence upon that too? What use is it to talk of this plague coming to us from a ship that came from Africa? Have you not read long ago together out of Leviticus 26:25, 'I shall bring a sword upon you, and avenge the quarrel of my covenant, and when you are assembled in the cities then will I bring the pestilence in the midst of you?' "

After this, having taken some little rest, she said, "O now is the day for opening the first question of the catechism; and if we were there, we should hear that, whether in death or life, a believer is Christ's, who has redeemed us by His own precious blood from the power of the devil." And then she quoted Romans 14:7-8, "'For none of us liveth unto himself, and none of us dieth unto himself. For whether we live, we live unto the Lord; and whether we die, we die unto the Lord; whether then we live or die, we are the Lord's.' Then be comforted, for whether I live or die, I am the Lord's. O why do you afflict yourselves thus? But what shall I say? With weeping I came into the world and with weeping I must go out again. O my dear parents, better is the day of my death than the day of my birth."

When she had thus encouraged her father and mother, she desired her father to pray with her and to request of the Lord that she might have a quiet and peaceable passage into another world.

After her father had prayed for her, he asked her whether he should send for the physician. She answered, "By no means, for now I am beyond the help of doctors."

"But," said he, "my child, we are to use the ordinary means appointed by the Lord for our help as long as we live, and let the Lord do as seems good in His eyes."

"But," said she, "give me the heavenly Physician. He is the only helper. Does not He say, 'Come unto Me all ye that are weary and heavy laden, and I will give you rest'? And does not He bid us call upon Him in the day of distress and He will deliver us and we shall glorify Him? Therefore, dear father, call upon Him yet again for me."

About this time a Christian friend came in to visit her, who was not a little comforted when he heard and saw so much of the grace of God living in a poor young thing, which could not but so far affect him as to draw tears of joy and admiration from him. And her deportment was so touching that he could not but acknowledge himself greatly edified and improved by her carriage and language.

That which was not the least observable in her was the ardent affection she had for the Holy Scriptures and her catechism, in which she was thoroughly instructed by the godly divines of the place where she lived, which she could not but own as one of the greatest mercies next to the Lord Christ. O how she blessed God for her catechism, and begged her father to go particularly to those ministers that had taken so much pains with her to instruct her in her catechism, and to thank them for her, a dying child, for their good in-

Example 11 63

structions, and to let them understand, for their encouragement to go on in that work of catechizing, how refreshing those truths were now to her in the hour of her distress. "O that sweet catechizing," said she "unto which I always resorted with gladness and attended without weariness."

She was much above the vanities of the world and took no pleasure at all in those things which usually take up the heart and time of young ones. She would say that she was grieved and ashamed, both for young and old, to see how mad they were upon vanity and how foolishly they spent their time.

She was not forgetful of the care and love of her master and mistress who taught her to read and work, but she desired that thanks might also be particularly given to them. Indeed, she thought she could never be thankful enough both to God and man for that kindness that she had experience of. But again and again, she desired to be sure to thank the minister that instructed her either by catechizing or preaching.

After some rest, her father asked her again how she did, and began to express somewhat of the satisfaction and joy that he had taken in her former diligence in her reading the Scriptures, writing, her dutifulness, and that great progress that she had made in the things of God. Upon hearing this, she humbly and sweetly desired to own God and His kindness in her godly education and said that she esteemed her holy education under such parents and minister as a greater portion than ten thousand guilders, "for thereby I have learned to comfort myself out of the Word of God, which the world besides could never have afforded."

Her father, perceiving that she was growing very

weak, said, "I perceive, child, that you are very weak."

"It is true, Sir," said she, "I feel my weakness increasing and I see your sorrow increasing too, which is a piece of my affliction. Be content, I pray you. It is the Lord who does it, and let you and I say with David, 'Let us fall into the Lord's hands, for His mercies are great.' "

She laid a great charge upon her parents not to be over-grieved for her after her death, urging that example of David upon them. "While his child was sick, he fasted and wept. But when it died, he washed his face, sat up and ate, and said, 'Can I bring him back again from death, I shall go to him but he shall not return to me.' So ought you to say after my death, our child is well, for we know it shall be well with them that trust in the Lord."

She laid a more particular and strict charge upon her mother, saying to her, "Dear mother, who has done so much for me, you must promise me one thing before I die: that you will not sorrow over-much for me. I speak thus to you because I am afraid of your great affliction. Consider what other losses have been. Remember Job. Forget not what Christ foretold, 'In the world you shall have tribulation, but be of good cheer, in Me you shall have peace.' And must the Apostles suffer so great tribulation, and must we suffer none? Did not Jesus Christ, my only Life and Savior, sweat drops of blood? Was He not in bitter agony, mocked, spit at, nailed to the cross, a spear thrust through His blessed side, and all this for my sake and on account of my sins? Did He not cry out, 'My God, My God, why hast Thou forsaken Me?' Did not Christ hang naked upon the cross to purchase for me the

Example 11   65

garments of salvation, and to clothe me with His righteousness, for there is salvation in no other name?"

Being very feeble and weak, she said, "Oh, if I
might quietly sleep in the bosom of Jesus! And that, till
then, He would strengthen me. Oh, that He would
take me into His arms as He did those little ones when
He said, 'Suffer the little children to come unto me,
for of such is the kingdom of heaven. And he took
them into His arms, and laid His hands on them and
blessed them!' I lie here as a child. O Lord, I am Thy
child. Receive me into Thy gracious arms. O Lord,
Grace! Grace, and not justice! For if Thou should
enter into judgment with me, I cannot stand; yes, for
none living should be just in Thy sight."

After this, she cried out, "Oh, how faint am I!" but
fearing lest she should dishearten her mother, she
said, "While there is life, there is hope. If it should
please the Lord to recover me, how careful would I be
to please you in my work and learning, and whatever
you should require of me!"

After this, the Lord again sent her strength. And
she labored to spend it all for Christ in awakening, edifying, and comforting those that were about her; but
her chief endeavor was to support her dear parents
from extraordinary sorrow and to comfort them out of
the Scriptures, telling them that she knew that all
things worked together for the good of those who love
God, even to those who are called according to His
purpose. "O God, establish me with Thy free Spirit!
'Who shall separate us from the love of Christ? I am
persuaded that neither life, nor death, nor angels, nor
principalities, nor powers, nor things present, nor
things to come, nor height, nor depth, nor any other

creature shall separate us from the love of God, which is towards us in Christ Jesus our Lord.' "

"'My sheep," said Christ, 'hear My voice, and I know them, and they follow Me, and I give unto them eternal life, and they shall never perish, and no man shall pluck them out of My hands. My Father who gave them Me is greater than all, and none shall pluck them out of My Father's hands.' " Thus, she seemed to obtain a holy confidence in God and an assurance of her state as to another world.

When she had refreshed herself a little with rest, she burst forth with abundance of joy and gladness of heart, with a holy triumph of faith, saying, "Death is swallowed up in victory, O death, where is thy sting? O grave where is thy victory? The sting of death is sin, and the strength of sin is the law; but thanks be to God, who hath given us the victory through our Lord and Savior Jesus Christ."

That she might better support her friends, she still insisted upon that which might take off some of their burden by urging the necessity of death, "We are from the earth, and to the earth we must return; dust is the mother of us all, the dust shall return to dust, from when it is, and the spirit to God who gave it."

Then she discoursed of the shortness of man's life. "Oh, what is the life of man! 'The days of man upon the earth are as the grass, and as the flowers of the field, so he flourisheth; the wind passeth over it, and it is gone, and his place knows him no more.' "

She further urged the sin and sorrow that attended unto us in this life, and the longer we live, the more we sin. "Now the Lord will free me from that sin and sorrow. We know not the thoughts of God, ye do we

Example 11   67

know so much that they are mercy and peace and give an expected end. But what shall I say? My life shall not continue long. I feel much weakness. O Lord, look upon me graciously, have pity upon my weak, distressed heart. I am oppressed. Undertake for me, that I may stand fast and overcome."

She was very frequent in spiritual ejaculations, and it was no small comfort to her that the Lord Christ prayed for her and promised to send His spirit to comfort her. "It is said," said she, "'I will pray the Father, and He shall give you another comforter.' O let Him not leave me! O Lord, continue with me till Thy work is finished."

She had very low and undervaluing thoughts of herself and her own righteousness. Or else what did her crying out in such language as that mean, "None but Christ! Without Thee, I can do nothing! Christ is the True Vine! Oh, let me be a branch of that Vine! What poor worms are we! O dear Father, how lame and halting we go in the ways of God and salvation! 'We know but in part. But when that which is perfect is come, then that which is imperfect shall be done away.' Oh, that I had attained to that now! But what are we ourselves? Not only weakness and nothingness, but weakness. For all the thoughts and imaginations of man's heart are only evil, and that continually. We are by nature children of wrath and are conceived and born in sin and unrighteousness. Oh, this wretched and vile thing—sin! But thanks be to God who has redeemed me from it."

She comforted herself and her father in that excellent Scripture, Romans 8:15-17, "'Ye have not received the spirit of bondage, again to fear, but ye have re-

ceived the spirit of adoption, by which we cry Abba
Father. It is the spirit that witnesseth with our spirits,
that we are the children of God; and if children, then
we are heirs, heirs of God, and joint heirs with Christ.'"

"You see, then, father," said she, "that I shall be a
fellow-heir with Christ who has said, 'In My Father's
house are many mansions. If it were not so, I would
have told you. I go to prepare a place for you, and if I
go to prepare a place for you, I will come again and
take you to Myself, that where I am there ye may be
also.' O Lord, take me to Thyself. Behold, dear
mother, He has prepared a place and dwelling for me."

"Yea, my dear child," said her mother," He shall
strengthen you with His Holy Spirit until He has fitted
and prepared you fully for that place which He has
provided for you."

"Yea, mother, it is said in Psalm 84, 'How lovely are
Thy tabernacles, O Lord of hosts. My soul doth thirst
for the courts of the Lord. One day in Thy courts is better than a thousand. Yea, I had rather be a door-keeper
in the house of God, than dwell in the tents of the
wicked.' Read that Psalm, dear mother, wherewith we
may comfort one another. As for me, I am more and
more spent and draw near my last hour."

Then she desired to be prayed with and begged
that the Lord would give her an easy passage.

After this, she turned to her mother and, with
much affection, she said, "Ah my dear and loving
mother, that which comes from the heart ordinarily
goes to the heart. Once more, come and kiss me before I leave you."

She was not a little concerned about the souls of
the rest of her relations, and particularly charged it

Example 11   69

upon her father to do what he could possibly to bring them in the ways of God. "O let my sister be trained up in the Scriptures and catechizing as I have been. I formerly wept for my sister, thinking that she would die before me, and now she weeps for me." And then she kissed her weeping sister. She also she took her young little sister in her arms, a child of six months old, kissed it with much affection, and spoke with many heart-breaking words both to her parents and the children.

Her father spoke to one who was near to take the poor little child away from her, from the hazard of that fiery distemper, and bid his daughter to give her to them, for he had already too much to bear. "Well father," said she, "did not God preserve the three children in the fiery furnace? And did you not teach me that Scripture, 'When thou passeth through the fire, thou shalt not be burnt, neither shall the flame kindle upon thee'? "

She had a very strong faith in the doctrine of the resurrection, and greatly solaced her soul with excellent Scriptures which speak of the happy state of believers as soon as their souls are separated from their bodies. And what she quoted out of the Scriptures, she excellently and suitably applied to her own use, incomparably above the common reach of her sex and age. 1 Corinthians 15:42 was a good support to her, "The body is sown in corruption, but it shall be raised incorruptible; it is sown in dishonor, it shall be raised in glory; it is sown in weakness, but it shall be raised in power."

And then she sweetly applied and took in this cordial. "Behold, thus it is, and thus it shall be with my mortal flesh, 'Blessed are the dead which die in the Lord, because they rest from their labors, and their works do follow them. The righteous perish, and no man layeth it to heart. And the upright are taken away, and no man regardeth it, that they are taken away from the evil to come, they shall enter into peace, they shall rest in their beds, every one who walketh in their uprightness.' Behold, now father, I shall rest and sleep in that bed-chamber."

Then she quoted Job 19:25-27, "'I know that my Redeemer liveth, and that he shall stand at the latter end upon the earth; and though after my skin, worms destroy this body, yet in my flesh shall I see God; whom I shall see for myself, and my eyes shall behold, and not another, though my reins be consumed within me.' Behold now, father, this very skin which you see, and this very flesh which you see, shall be raised up again. And these very eyes, which now are so dim, shall, on that day see and behold my dear and precious Redeemer. Though the worms eat up my flesh, yet, with these eyes, shall I behold God, even I myself, and not another for me."

Then she quoted John 5:28, "'Marvel not at this, for the hour is coming in which all that are in their graves shall hear His voice, and come forth; those that have done good unto the resurrection of life.' See, father, I shall rise in that day, and then I shall behold my Redeemer; then shall He say, 'Come ye blessed of My Father, inherit the kingdom prepared for you before the beginning of the world.'

"'Behold now I live, yet not I, but Christ liveth in me, and the life that I now live in the flesh is by the faith of the Son of God, who loved me and gave

Example 11   71

Himself for me.' I am saved, and that not of myself, 'it is the gift of God, not of works, lest any man should boast.'

"My dear parents, now we must shortly part, my speech fails me, pray to the Lord for a quiet close to my combat."

Her parents replied, "Ah, our dear child! How sad is that to us, that we must part!"

She answered, "I go to heaven, and there we shall find one another again. I go to Jesus Christ."

Then she comforted herself to think of seeing her precious brother and sister again in glory. "I go to my brother Jacob, who did so much cry and call upon God to the last moment of his breath; and to my little sister, who was but three years old when she died; who, when we asked her whether she would die, answered, 'Yes, if it is the Lord's will. I will go to my little brother, if it is the Lord's will, or I will stay with my mother, if it be the Lord's will. But I know that I shall die and go to heaven and to God.' Oh, see how so small a babe had so much given it to behave itself every way, and in all things, so submissively to the will of God, as if it had no will of its own: 'But if it be the will of God; if it please God.' Nothing for her but what was the will and pleasure of God. And, therefore, dear father and mother, give the Lord thanks for His free and rich grace, and then I shall the more gladly be gone. Be gracious then, O Lord unto me also. Be gracious to me. Wash me thoroughly from my unrighteousness and cleanse me from my sin."

After this, her spirit was refreshed with the sense of the pardon of her sins, which made her to cry out, "Behold, God has washed away my sins. O how I long to die! The Apostle said, 'In this body we earnestly sigh and groan, longing for our house which is in heaven, that we may be clothed therewith.' Now, I also lie here sighing and longing for that dwelling which is above. In the last sermon which I heard, or ever shall hear, I heard this, which is matter of great comfort unto me."

Then she repeated several notable Scriptures which were quoted in that sermon. Afterward, she desired to be prayed with and put petitions into their mouths, namely, that all her sins might be forgiven, that she might have more abundant faith, the assurance of it, and the comfort of that assurance, and the continuation and strength of the comfort according as her necessity should require. Afterwards she prayed herself and continued some time.

When her prayers were ended, she called to her father and mother and demanded of them whether she had at any time angered or grieved them or done any thing that did not become her. She then begged them to forgive her.

They answered her that if all children had carried themselves so to their parents as she had done, there would be less grief and sorrow on all hands than there is. She said, "If any such thing had escaped from you, we would forgive it with all our hearts. You have done as becomes a good child."

Her heart being comforted with her peace with God and her parents, she began to dispose of her books. Particularly, she entreated her mother to keep Mr. De Wit's catechetical lectures as long as she lived for her sake, and "Let my little sister have my other books in remembrance of me."

Then she said that she felt her chest exceedingly

Example 11   73

pained, by which she knew that her end was very nigh. Her father spake to her as he was able, telling her that the Lord would be her strength in the hour of her necessity.

"Yea," said she, "The Lord is my shepherd. Although I pass through the valley of the shadow of death, I will not fear, for 'Thou art with me, Thy rod and Thy staff, they comfort me.' And it is said, 'The sufferings of this present life are not worthy to be compared with the glory that shall be revealed in us.' Shall I not suffer and endure, seeing that my glorious Redeemer was pleased to suffer so much for me? Oh, how was He mocked and crowned with thorns that He might purchase a crown of righteousness for us! And that is the crown of which Paul spoke when he said, 'I have fought the good fight, I have finished my course, I have kept the faith, henceforth there is laid up for me a crown of righteousness, which the Lord, the righteous judge shall give unto me in that day—and not to me only but to all who love His appearing.'

"'Ye are bought with a price, therefore glorify God with your souls and bodies, which are His.' Must I not, then, exalt and bless Him while I have a being, who has bought me with His blood? 'Surely He hath borne our griefs, and took our infirmities, and we esteemed Him smitten, stricken of God. But He was wounded for our transgressions, and bruised for our sins. The chastisement of our peace was upon Him, and by His stripes we are healed, and the Lord laid upon Him the iniquity of us all.' 'Behold the Lamb of God that taketh away the sins of the world.' That lamb is Jesus Christ who has satisfied for my sins. So said Paul, 'Ye are washed, ye are sanctified, ye are justified in the name of Lord Jesus, and through the Spirit of our God.'

"My end is now very near. Now I shall put on white raiment and be clothed before the Lamb, that spotless Lamb, and with His spotless righteousness. Now are the angels making ready to carry my soul before the throne of God. 'These are they who are come out of great tribulation, who have washed their robes and made them white in the blood of the lamb.' "

She spoke this with a dying voice, but full of spirit and the power of faith.

Her lively assurance she further uttered in the words of the Apostle, "We know that if this earthly house of our tabernacle be dissolved, we have one which is built of God, which is eternal in the heavens; for in this we sigh for our house, which is in heaven, that we may be clothed therewith."

"There, father, you see that my body is this tabernacle which now shall be broken down. My soul shall not part from it, and shall be taken up into that heavenly paradise, in that heavenly Jerusalem. There shall I dwell and go no more out, but sit and sing, 'Holy, holy, holy, is the Lord God of hosts, the Lord of Sabaoth!' "

Her last words were these, "O Lord God, into Thy hands I commit my spirit! O Lord be gracious, be merciful to me, a poor sinner!" And here she fell asleep.

She died the first of September, 1664, between seven and eight in the evening, in the 14th year of her age, having obtained that which she so often entreated of the Lord—a quiet and easy departure, and the end of her faith and salvation of her soul.

Example 12

Of the excellent conduct of a child upon his death-bed,
when but seven years old.

Jacob Bicks, the brother of Susannah Bicks, was
born in Leyden and had a religious education under
his godly parents which the Lord was pleased to
sanctify to his conversion and, by it, lay in excellent
provisions to live upon in an hour of distress.

This sweet little child was visited of the Lord by a
very sore sickness three or four weeks before his sister,
of whose life and death we have given you some
account already. In his distemper, he was, for the most
part, very sleepy and drowsy till near his death, but
when he awoke, he was wont to be much engaged in
prayer.

Once, when his parents had been praying with him,
they asked him again if they should send for a
physician? "No," said he, "I will have the doctor no
more. The Lord will help me. I know He will take me
to Himself and then He shall help all."

"Ah my dear child," said his father, "that grieves my
heart."

"Well," said the child, "father, let us pray, and the
Lord shall be near for my helper."

When his parents had prayed with him again, he
said, "Come now, dear father and mother, and kiss me,
for I know that I shall die. Farewell, dear father and
mother, farewell dear sister, farewell all. Now shall I go

to heaven unto God and Jesus Christ, and the holy angels. Father, know you not what is said by Jeremiah: 'Blessed is he who trusteth in the Lord'? Now I trust in Him, and He will bless me. And in 1 John 2 it is said, 'Little children love not the world, for the world passeth away.' Away, then, all that is in the world. Away with all my pleasant things in the world. Away with my dagger, for where I go there is nothing to do with daggers and swords. Men shall not fight there but praise God. Away with all my books. There shall I know sufficiently and be learned in all things of true wisdom without books."

His father, being touched to hear his child speak at this rate, could not well tell what to say but, "My dear child, the Lord will be near you and uphold you."

"Yea, father," said he, "the Apostle Peter said, 'God resisteth the proud, but He giveth grace to the humble.' I shall humble myself under the mighty hand of God, and He shall help me and lift me up."

"O my dear child," said his father, "have you so strong a faith?"

"Yes," said the child, "God has given me so strong a faith upon Himself through Jesus Christ that the devil himself shall flee from me, for it is said, 'He who believeth in the Son hath everlasting life, and he hath overcome the wicked one.' Now I believe in Jesus Christ my Redeemer, and He will not leave nor forsake me, but shall I sing, Holy, holy, holy, is the Lord of Sabaoth."

Then, with a short word of prayer, "Lord be merciful to me, a poor sinner," he quietly breathed out his soul and sweetly slept in Jesus when he was about seven years.

Example 13

Of one who began to look towards heaven when he was very young, with many eminent passages of his life and joyful death when he was 11 and three-quarters years old.

John Harvey was born in London, in the year 1654. His father was a Dutch merchant. He was piously educated under his virtuous mother and soon began to suck in divine things with no small delight.

The first thing very observable in him was that, when he was two years and eight months old, he could speak as well as other children usually do at five years.

His parents, judging that he was then a little too young to send out to school, let him have his liberty to play a little about home. But, instead of playing, he found a school of his own accord near by, went to a school mistress, and entreated her to teach him to read. And so he went, for some time, to school without the knowledge of his parents, made a very great progress in his learning, and was able to read distinctly before most children are able to know their letters.

He was inclined to ask many serious and weighty questions about matters which concerned his soul and eternity. His mother being greatly troubled upon the death of one of his uncles, this child came to his mother and said, "Mother, though my uncle is dead, does not the Scripture say that he must rise again? Yea, and I must die, and so must everybody, and it will not be long before Christ will come to judge the world and then we shall see one another again. I pray, mother, do not weep so much." This grave counsel he gave his mother when he was not quite five years old, by which her sorrow for her brother was turned into admiration at her child, and she was made to sit silent and quiet under that smarting stroke.

After this, his parents moved to Aberdeen in Scotland and settled their child under an able schoolmaster there whose custom was, upon the Lord's day morning, to examine his young scholars concerning the sermons that they had heard the former Lord's day, and to add some questions which might try the understanding and knowledge of his students. His master was often amazed at this child's answers and took an opportunity to go to his mother to thank her for instructing her son so well. But she replied that he improved in his understanding not only by her instructions, but by his own reading and observation.

He was a child who was extraordinarily inquisitive, full of good questions, and very careful to observe and remember what he heard. He had a great hatred of whatever he knew to be displeasing to God, and he was so greatly concerned for the honor of God that he would be much displeased if any gross sins were committed before him. He had a deep sense of the worth of souls and was not a little grieved when he saw anyone do that which he knew was dangerous to their souls.

One day, seeing one of his near relations come into his father's house distempered with drink, as he thought, he quickly went very seriously to him and wept over him that he should so offend God and hazard his soul, and begged him to spend his time better

Example 13   79

than in drinking and gaming. And this he did without any instruction from his parents but from an inward principle of grace and love to God and souls, it is verily believed.

When he was at play with other children, he would be oftentimes putting in some word to keep them from naughty talk or wicked actions. And if anyone took the Lord's name in vain or anything unbecoming a good child they would soon hear about it from him. Nay, once hearing a boy speak very profanely, and that after two or three admonitions, he would not forbear nor go out of his company either. He was so transported with zeal that he could not forbear falling upon him to beat him. But his mother chiding him for it, he said that he could not endure to hear the name of God so abused by a wretched boy. This is observed not to vindicate the act but to take notice of his zeal.

He was a child who took great delight in the company of good men, especially ministers and scholars. And if he had any leisure time, he would improve it by visiting such whose discourse might make him wiser and better. When he was in their society, he made sure that his talk was more like a Christian and a scholar than a child.

One day after school time was over, he paid Mr. Andrew Kent, one of the ministers of Aberdeen, a visit and asked him several solid questions. But the good man asked him some questions out of his catechism, and, finding him not as ready in the answers as he should have been, Mr. Kent reproved him a little and told him that he must be sure to get his catechism perfectly by heart. The child took the reproof very well and went home and set very closely to his catechism and never left it till he got it by heart. And not only so, but he would be enquiring into the sense and meaning of it.

He was so greatly taken with his catechism that he was not content to learn it himself, but put others to learning it also, especially those who were nearest to him. He could not be satisfied till he had persuaded the servants to learn it, and when they were at work he would be still following them with some good question or other so that the child seemed to be taken up with the thoughts of his soul, God's honor, and the good of others.

He was a conscientious observer of the Lord's day, spending all the time either in secret prayer, reading the Scriptures and good books, learning his catechism, hearing the Word of God, or attending to public duties. And he was not only careful in the performance of those duties himself but was ready to put all that he knew upon a strict observation of the Lord's day, and was exceeding grieved at the profanation of it. One Lord's day, a servant of his father's, going out of the house upon an extraordinary occasion to fetch something that was wanted, he took it so bitterly that he could scarce be pacified because that holy day was so abused, as he judged, in his father's house.

When he was between six and seven years old, it pleased God to afflict him with sore eyes, which was no small grief to him because it kept him from school which he loved as well as many boys do their play. And, what was worse, he was commanded by the doctor not to read any book whatever at home. But, oh, how was this poor child grieved that he might not have liberty to read the holy Scriptures! And, for all their charge,

Example 13   81

he would get by himself and stand by the window and read the Bible and other good books. Yea, he was so greedy of reading the Scriptures and took so much delight in them, that he would scarcely allow himself time to dress himself, for reading the Word of God was his great delight. Yea, though he had been beaten for studying so much, yet, judging it God's command that he should give himself up to reading, he could not be beat off from it till he was so bad that he would likely never recover his sight again.

It was his practice to be much by himself in secret prayer. And he was careful to manage that work so that it might be as secret as it possibly could be, but his frequency and constancy made it to be easily observed! One time, one, having a great mind to know what this sweet babe prayed for, got into a place near him and heard him very earnestly praying for the Church of God, desiring that the kingdom of the gospel might be spread over the whole world, that the kingdom of grace might more and more come into the hearts of God's people, and that the kingdom of glory might be hastened. He was inclined to continue half an hour, sometimes an hour, upon his knees.

He was much above the vanities that most children are taken with and was, indeed, too much above this world we live in.

He was very humble and modest and was by no means affected by fineness in apparel but hated anything more than bare necessities either in clothes or diet. When he perceived either his brother or sister pleased with their new clothes, he would, with a great deal of gravity, reprove their folly. And when his reproof signified little, he would bewail their vanity.

Once he had a new suit brought him which, when he looked on, he found some ribbons at the knee at which he was grieved, asking his mother whether these things would keep him warm.

"No, child," said his mother.

"Why, then," said he, "do you allow them to be put here? You are mistaken if you think such things please me. I do not doubt but that some, who are better than us, may lack the money that this cost you to buy them bread."

He would entreat his mother to have a care of gratifying a proud humor in his brother and sisters. He told them of the danger of pride, and how little reason they had to be proud of that which was their shame. For, said he, "If it had not been for sin, we should have no need of clothes."

At leisure times, he would be talking to his schoolfellows about the things of God and urging upon them the necessity of a holy life. This text he much spoke about to them, "'The axe is laid to the root of the tree, and every tree that bringeth not forth good fruit, is hewn down and cast into the fire.' Every mother's child of us that does not bring forth the fruit of good works shall shortly be cut down with the axe of God's wrath and cast down into the fire of hell." And this he spoke like one that believed and felt the power of what he spake, and not with the least visibility of a childish levity of spirit. This was when he was between seven and eight years old. And if he perceived any children unconcerned about their souls, he would be greatly troubled at it.

After this, his parents moved not far from London,

Example 13   83

where he continued till that dreadful year 1665.[1] He
was sent to the Latin school where he soon made considerable progress and was greatly beloved of his master. The school was his beloved place and learning his
recreation. He was never taught to write, but took it of
his own ingenuity.

He was exceeding dutiful to his parents and never
in the least disputed their commands except when he
thought they might cross the command of God, as in
the formentioned business of reading the Scriptures
when his eyes were so bad.

He was exceedingly contented with any mean diet
and, to be sure, he would not touch a bit of anything
till he had begged God's blessing upon it.

He put his brother and sister upon their duties and
observed whether they performed them or not. And
when he saw any neglect, he would soon warn them. If
he saw any of them take a spoon into their hands before he had craved a blessing, he said, "That is just like
a hog, indeed!"

His sister was afraid of the darkness and would
sometimes cry upon this account. He told her, "You
must fear God more, and then you need be afraid of
nothing."

He would humbly put his near relations upon their
duty, the need to mind the concerns of their souls and
eternity with more seriousness and life, and to have a
care of doing that which was for the dishonor of God

---

[1] The Great Plague of London, in which approximately one out of
seven of the city's population died, took place in 1665. The bacterial
disease, transmitted by fleas from rats, often proved fatal before the
development of modern antibiotics.

and the hazard of the soul.

He was of a compassionate and charitable disposition. He was very pitiful to the poor or any that were in distress, but his greatest pity was to poor souls. As well as he could, he would be putting children, play-fellows, servants, and neighbors upon minding their precious souls.

I cannot omit one notable instance of his true charity. A certain Turk was, by the providence of God, cast into the place where he lived, which this sweet child hearing of had a great pity to his soul and studied how he might be any way instrumental to do it good. At last, finding a man who understood the language of the Turk, he used means to get them together which he at last procured. The first thing that he did was to put his friend upon discoursing with the Turk about his principles, whether he acknowledged a Deity. The Turk owning that he did, the next thing he inquired was what he thought of the Lord Jesus Christ. At this, the Turk was troubled, put off the discourse, and said that he was thirsty and hungry. The child, being informed of this by the interpreter, immediately went to a brewhouse near at hand, his own house being far off, and entreated the master of it to give him some beer for the Turk. The argument he used was this, "Sir, here is a poor stranger that is thirsty; we know not where we may be cast before we die." He then went to another place and begged food for him, using the same argument as before. But his friends, hearing of it, were angry with him, but he told them he did it for a poor stranger that was far from home, and he did it that he might think the better of the Christians and the Christian religion.

Example 13   85

He would have a savory word to say to every one that he conversed with to put them in mind of the worth of Christ, their souls and their nearness to eternity—insomuch that good people took no small pleasure in his company. The tailor that made his clothes would keep them the longer before he brought them home, that he might have the benefit of his spiritual and Christian society and more frequent visits.

When he was about ten years old, he bewailed the miserable condition of the generality of mankind that were utterly estranged from God. Though they called Him Father, yet they were his children only by creation and not by any likeness they had to God or interest in Him.

Thus, he continued walking in the ways of God, engaged in reading, praying, hearing the Word of God, and spiritual discourse, revealing thereby his serious thoughts of eternity.

He had an earnest desire, if it might be the Lord's good pleasure, to give himself up to the Lord in the work of the ministry, if he should live, and this out of a dear love to Christ and souls.

He was, next to the Bible, most taken with reading of the reverend Mr. [Richard] Baxter's works, especially his *Saint's Everlasting Rest;*[2] and, truly, the thoughts of that rest and eternity seemed to swallow up all other thoughts. He lived in a constant preparation for it and looked more like one that was ripe for glory

---

[2] Richard Baxter (1615-1696), Puritan divine, published his *The Saint's Everlasting Rest*, his most famous work, in 1650. It is contained in volume 3 of The Practical Works of Richard Baxter, reprinted in 1990 by Soli Deo Gloria.

than an inhabitant of this lower world.

When he was about eleven years and three quarters old, his mother's house was visited with the plague. His eldest sister was the first that was visited with this distemper and, when they were praying for her, he would sob and weep bitterly.

As soon as he perceived his sister was dead, he said, "The will of the Lord be done, blessed be the Lord. Dear mother, you must do as David did after the child was dead. He went and refreshed himself, and quietly submitted to the will of God."

The rest of the family held well for about 14 days, which time he spent in religious duties and preparing for his death. But still his favorite book was *The Saint's Rest*, which he read with great attention, gathering many observations out of it for his own use. He wrote several divine meditations of his own upon several subjects. But that which seemed most admirable was a meditation on the excellency of Christ. He was never well now, except when he was immediately engaged in the service of God.

At 14 days end, he was taken sick, at which he seemed very patient and cheerful. Yet sometimes he would say that his pain was great.

His mother, looking upon his brother, shook her head, at which he asked if his brother were in danger. She answered, "Yea, child." He asked again whether she thought him so. She answered nothing, "Well," said he, "I pray, let me have Mr. Baxter's book that I may read a little more of eternity before I go into it."

His mother told him that he was not able to read. He said that he was, however. "Then pray by me and for me."

Example 13   87

His mother answered that she was so full of grief
that she could not pray now, but she desired to hear
him pray his last prayer.

His mother asked him whether he was willing to die
and leave her. He answered, "Yes, I am willing to leave
you and go to my heavenly Father."

His mother answered, "Child, if you only had an assurance of God's love, I would not be so troubled."

He answered and said to his mother, "I am assured,
dear mother, that my sins are forgiven, that I shall go
to heaven. For there stood an angel by me that told me
I should quickly be in glory."

At this, his mother burst forth into tears. "O
mother," said he, "did you but know what joy I feel,
you would not weep but rejoice! I tell you, I am so full
of comfort that I cannot tell you how I am. O mother, I
shall presently have my head in my father's bosom, and
I shall be there where the 'four and twenty elders cast
down their crowns and sing hallelujah, glory and praise
to Him that sits upon the throne, and unto the Lamb
for ever!' "

Upon this, his speech began to fail him, but his
soul seemed still to be taken up with glory. Nothing
now grieved him but the sorrow that he saw his mother
to be in for his death. A little to divert his mother, he
asked what she had for supper. But presently, in a kind
of divine rapture, he cried out, "Oh, what a sweet
supper have I making ready for me in glory!"

But feeling all this rather increased than allayed his
mother's grief, he was more troubled and asked her
what she meant thus to offend God. "Know you not
that it is the hand of the Almighty? 'Humble yourself
under the mighty hand of God,' lay yourself in the

dust, and kiss the rod of God, and let me see you do it in token of your submission to the will of God and bow before Him." Upon which, raising himself up a little, he gave a lowly bow and spoke no more, but went cheerfully and triumphantly to rest in the bosom of Jesus.

A Token for the Children of New England

Or some examples of children in whom the fear of
God was remarkably budding before they died in
several parts of New England; published for
the encouragement of piety
in other children.

by

Cotton Mather

Preface

If the children of New England should not, with an early piety, set themselves to know and serve the Lord Jesus Christ, the God of their Fathers, they will be condemned not only by the examples of pious children in other parts of the world, the published and printed accounts whereof have been brought over hither. But there have been exemplary children in the midst of New England itself who will rise up against them for their condemnation. It would be a very profitable thing to our children, and highly acceptable to all the godly parents of the children, if, in imitation of the excellent Janeway's *Token for Children*, there were made a true collection of notable things exemplified in the lives and deaths of many among us whose childhood has been signalized for what is virtuous and laudable.

In the church history of New England is to be found the lives of many eminent persons, among whose eminencies not the least was their hearing of the Lord from their youth, and their being loved by the Lord when they were children.

But among the many other instances of a childhood and youth delivered from vanity by serious religion which New England has afforded, these few have particularly been preserved.

Example 1

John Clap of Scituate, Massachusetts was little more than 13 years old when he died; but it might very truly be said of him that, while he was yet young, he began to seek after the God of his father. From his infancy, he discovered a singular delight in the Holy Scriptures whereby he was made wise unto salvation. And he also made himself yet further amiable by his obedience to his parents and his courtesy to all his neighbors. As he grew up, he signalized his concern for eternity not only by his diligent attendance upon both public and private catechising, but also by the like attendance on the ministry of the Word, which he would ponder, apply, and confer about with much discretion of soul, and pray for the good effect thereon upon his own soul. Yea, 'twas observable in him even from his childhood that after he began to speak reasonably, he would both affectionately regard the family prayers and, likewise, both morning and evening, with a most unwearied constancy, recommend himself by his own prayers unto the mercies of God.

Arriving higher into his age, he was very conscientious of his duty both to God and man. And he was particularly careful of his father's business, which now became his own calling. At work with his father in the field, he would frequently be propounding of questions, by the answers of which he might be promoted in the knowledge of God. And,

Example 1   93

at the seasons which others usually employ to vain purpose, he would be abounding in the exercises of devotion. But of all the praiseworthy things to be seen in him, he was exemplary for nothing more than his endeavors in preparation for, and sanctification of, the Lord's Day. Yea, his parents have affirmed that for a year or two before he died, they never heard an unprofitable word come out of his mouth. But he would often bewail the idle, trifling, vain discourses of other people.

About a year and a half before he died, the good Spirit of God blessed him with yet a more thorough conviction of his misery by reason of sin both original and actual; whence, though he had been such a pattern of innocency, yet he would aggravate his own sinfulness with lamentations truly extraordinary. And for his relief against the terrors of God, wherewith he was now distracted, he was brought unto an utter despair of his own righteousnesses and abilities. But in this condition, he came to adore the grace of God in offering a Jesus who is able to save unto the uttermost. In his longings to enjoy the love of God through Jesus, he was like the hart panting after the water-brooks.

The wounds of the Spirit were accompanied with a languishing and consuming of his flesh. Yet, with great patience, he endured the hand of God, and he followed the Lord with prayers, with cries, with tears for the manifestation of the divine love unto him.

It was also observed and admired that, when he was abroad at the public worship, in the time of his weakness, he would stand the whole time of the long exercises and be so affectionately attentive that one might see every sentence uttered in those exercises make some impression upon him. The best Christians in the place professed themselves ashamed by the fervency of this young disciple. In days of public humiliations or thanksgivings kept with regard unto the general circumstances of the country, he would bear his part with such a sense of the public troubles or mercies as argued more than a common measure of a public spirit in him.

The minister of the place, visiting him after sickness had confined him, found him in extreme dejection of soul. His very body shook through his fear lest the day of grace was over for him. Yet he justified God, though he should be forever cast among the damned. But yet his fears were accompanied with hopes in the all-sufficient merits of the blessed Jesus, in which hopes he continued using all the means of grace, according to his capacity, and lamenting after those whereof he was not capable.

A month before he died, he kept to his bed. The first fortnight whereof he was very comfortless, yet very patient, abounding all this while in gracious admonitions unto other young people, that they would be concerned for their own eternal salvation. And you should not now have heard him complain that he lacked health and ease—though he did so— but that he wanted faith, peace, and Christ, yet expressing a profound submission to the will of God. But in the last fortnight of his life, this poor child of God had his weary soul more comfortably satisfied with the promises of the New Covenant. God filled him with a marvelous assurance of His love and so sealed him with His own Spirit that he rejoiced with

Example 1   95

joy unspeakable and full of glory. He would often be saying, "Whom have I in heaven but Thee? And there is none on earth that I desire besides Thee. My flesh and My heart faileth, but God is the strength of my heart, and my portion forever!" And, "I know that my Redeemer lives, and that He shall stand at the latter day upon the earth." And, "If I live, I shall live unto the Lord; if I die, I shall die unto the Lord; and whether I live or die, I am the Lord's." And, "When Christ, who is my life, shall appear, then shall I also appear with Him in glory." He would profess that his communion with the Lord Jesus Christ was inexpressible. And the spectators judged his consolations to be as great as could be borne in a mortal body.

Being now asked whether the thoughts of dying troubled him not, he replied, "No, death is no terror to me because Christ has taken away my sin, which is the sting of death." But being asked whether he was willing to live, he answered, "I am willing to submit to the will of God. But if God has appointed me to life, I desire I may live to His glory." And being asked whether God had put out of doubt his interests in a dying and rising Jesus, he returned, "Yes, and God has fully answered my desires. I am now going to a thousand times better world." He told his mother, "I love you as dearly as my own life, yet I would rather die and be with Christ."

He continued six days with his teeth so shut that they could not be opened. For the first three days and nights, he took no sustenance. Afterwards, though this but seldom, he sucked between his teeth nothing but a little cold water, in which time they that laid their ears to his lips could overhear him continually expressing his comfort in God. But just before his death, his teeth were opened. Then he would often say, "Oh, how precious is the blood of Christ. It is worth more than a thousand worlds!" and often pray, "Come, Lord Jesus, come quickly!" At last, he gave up himself to God in those words, "Lord Jesus, receive my spirit." He desired his mother to turn his face unto the wall, whereupon she said, "John, do you now remember Hezekiah's turning his face unto the wall?" He said, "Yes, I do remember it." And as she turned him in her arms, he quietly breathed his soul into the arms of his blessed Savior.

(Extracted out of the account written and printed by Mr. Witheril and Mr. Baker, minister of Scituate; and prefaced by Mr. Urian Oakes [1631-1681, a Puritan minister, poet, and president of Harvard College] who takes that occasion to say of this John Clap, "He was a young old man, full of grace, though not full of days.")

Example 2

Mr. Thomas Thornton, the aged and faithful pastor of Yarmouth, was blessed with a daughter named Priscilla who at the age of eleven left this world, having first given demonstrations of an exemplary piety.

She was remarkably grave, devout, and serious, very inquisitive about the matters of eternity and, in her particular calling, very diligent. She was, nevertheless, troubled with sore temptations and exercises about the state of her own soul. The anguish of her spirit about her body of death caused her to pour out many tears and prayers. And she pressed that some other pious children of her acquaintance might, with her, keep a day of humiliation together that (as she expressed it) they might get power against their sinful natures. But it pleased God at length to bless the words of her godly mother for the quieting of her mind. It was her singular happiness that she had such godly parents; but it was her opinion and expression, "We trust too much to the prayers of our parents, whereas we should pray for ourselves."

At last she fell mortally sick. In the beginning of her sickness, she was afraid of dying. For, said she, "I know of no promise to encourage me." She could not but own that she had in some measure walked with God. Yet she complained that she had not found God meeting her in her prayers and making her heart willing to be at His disposal and that the pride of her heart now lay as a load upon it. She owned that she had many thoughts of Jesus Christ, and that it grieved her that she had sinned against Him who had done and died for her.

But many days were not past before she could profess herself willing to die, with some assurance of her then going to eternal blessedness. Many thanks and much love she now rendered to one of her superiors, declaring that it was because they had curbed and restrained her from sinful vanities. And she said, "Were I now to choose my company, it should be among the people of God. I see plainly that they are the only company." She was not without her conflicts in this time, wherein one of her speeches was, "Damnation is the worst thing of all, but Christ is of all the best. I find that Christ is to me wisdom, righteousness, sanctification, and redemption."

She told her father she knew she was made up of all manner of sin. But, said she, "I hope God has humbled me, and pardoned me in the merits of the Lord Jesus Christ." Unto her affectionate mother she said, "Mother, why do you weep when I am well in my soul? Will you mourn when I am so full of joy? I pray, rejoice with me."

When she was extremely spent, she said to her parent, "Oh, my father, I have been much troubled by Satan, but I find Christ is too hard for him and sin and all." She now said, "I know that I shall die." Being asked whether she was afraid of death, with a sweet smile she replied, "No, not I. Christ is better than life." And so she continued in a joyful frame

Example 2   99

until she died, a little before which, it being the
Lord's Day, she asked what time of day it was. When
they had told her that it was three o'clock, she
replied, "What, is the Sabbath almost done? Well, my
eternal Sabbath is going to begin, wherein I shall
enjoy all felicity and sing hallelujahs to all eternity."
And, hereupon, she quickly fell asleep in the Lord.

Example 3

Mr. Nathanael Mather [Cotton Mather's brother] died October 17, 1688, at the age of nineteen, an instance of more than common learning and virtue. On his grave stone at Salem there are these words deservedly inscribed, "The ashes of an hard student, a good scholar, and a great Christian."

He was one who used an extraordinary diligence to obtain skill in the several arts that make an accomplished scholar, but he was more diligent in his endeavors to become an experienced Christian.

With much solemnity, he entered into covenant with God when he was about 14 years old. And afterwards he renewed that solemn action in such form as this:

"I renounce all the vanities and wretched idols and evil courses of the world.

I choose, and will ever have, the great God for my best good, my last end, my only Lord. He shall be the only one, in the glorifying and enjoying of whom shall be my welfare and in the serving of whom shall be my work.

I will ever be rendering unto the Lord Jesus Christ my proper acknowledgments as unto my Priest, my Prophet, my King, and the Physician of my soul. I will ever be studying what is my duty in these things and, where I find myself to fall short, I will ever count it my grief and shame and betake

Example 3   101

myself to the blood of the everlasting covenant.

Now, humbly imploring the grace of the Mediator to be sufficient for me, as a further solemnity, I hereunto subscribe my name with both heart and hand."

Having done this, for the rest of his life he walked with watchfulness and exactness.

One of the directories which he drew up for himself was this:

"Oh, that I might lead a spiritual life. Wherefore let me regulate my life by the Word of God and by such Scripture as these:

1. For regulating my thoughts, Jeremiah 4:14, Isaiah 55:7; and Psalm 104:34.

2. For regulating my affections, Colossians 3:2, 5 and Galatians 5:24.

    For my delight, Psalm 1:2.

    For my joy, Philippians 4:4.

    For my desire, Isaiah 2:6; 8:9.

    For my love, Matthew 22:37.

    For my hatred, Psalm 97:10.

    For my fear, Luke 12:4-5.

    For my hope, Psalm 39:7.

    For my trust, Psalm 62:8 and Isaiah 26:4.

3. For regulating my speech, Ephesians 4:29; Colossians 4:6; and Deuteronomy 6:6-7.

4. For regulating my work, Titus 3:8; 1 Timothy 5:10; and Matthew 5:47."

Another of his directories was formed into a hymn:

Lord, what shall I return unto Him from whom all my mercies flow?
>   *(1.) To me to live, it Christ shall be,*
>   *For all I do I'll do for Thee.*
>   *(2.) My question shall be oft beside,*
>   *How Thou mayst most be glorified.*
>   *(3.) I will not any creature love;*
>   *But in the love of Thee above.*
>   *(4.) Thy will I will embrace for mine;*
>   *And every management of thine shall please me.*
>   *(5.) A conformity to Thee shall be my aim and eye.*
>   *(6.) Ejaculations shall ascend not seldom from me.*
>   *(7.) I'll attend occasional reflections and*
>   *Turn all to gold that comes to hand.*
>   *(8.) And in particular among my cares,*
>   *I'll try to make my tongue a tree of life*
>   *By speaking all as be accountable who shall.*
>   *(9.) But last, nay first of all, I will*
>   *Thy Son my surety make and still*
>   *Implore Him that He would me bless,*
>   *With strength as well as righteousness.*

He would also keep whole days of prayer and praise by himself. And he would set himself to consider much on that question, "What shall I do for God?"

He was much in meditation, and often wrote the chief heads of his meditation. He would read the Scripture with a note and a wish fetched out of every verse. At night he would ask:

Example 3   103

1. What has God's mercy to me been this day?
2. What has my carriage to God been this day?
3. If I die this night, is my immortal spirit safe?

Many more such excellent things are in the history of his life (various times printed at London) reported of him.

Example 4

Ann Greenough, the daughter of Mr. William Greenough, left the world when she was but five years old, and yet gave astonishing discoveries of a regard unto God, Christ, and her own soul before she went away. When she heard anything about the Lord Jesus Christ, she would be strangely transported and ravished in her spirit at it, and she had an unspeakable delight in catechizing. She would put strange questions about eternal things, and make answers herself that were extremely pertinent.

Once particularly she asked, "Are not we dead in sin?" and presently added, "but I will take this away. The Lord Jesus Christ shall make me alive." She was very frequent and constant in secret prayer and could not, with any patience, be interrupted in it. She told her gracious mother that she there prayed for her! And she was covetous of being with her mother when she imagined such duties to be going forward.

When she fell sick at last of a consumption, she would not be diverted by any sports from the thoughts of death, wherein she took such pleasure that she did not care to hear of anything else. And, if she were asked whether she were willing to die, she would cheerfully reply, "Ah, by all means, that I may go to the Lord Jesus Christ."

Example 5

At Boston, on March 12, 1694, there died one Daniel Williams, in the 18th year of his age.

There was a collection made of some of his dying speeches.

Being asked whether he loved God, he replied, "Yes, I love him dearly, for Lord, whom have I in heaven but Thee?"

He said, "God has promised that they who seek Him early shall find Him. Ever since I was a child, I dedicated myself to seek and serve the Lord. Though I have not had so much time as others, yet that little time which I had, I spent in waiting on and wrestling with God in prayer. I said, 'I will not let Thee go till Thou hast blessed me.' "

Seeing some of his relations weep he said, "Why do you cry, when I am ready to sing for joy?"

They said that they did not know how to part with him. To which he replied, "Are you not willing I should go to my heavenly Father? I shall quickly be with my heavenly Father, and with his holy angels, where they are singing Hallelujahs. It's better being there than here. When I am there, I shan't wish myself here in this troublesome world again. I have a desire to depart and be with Christ, which is best of all."

He was much concerned for poor perishing souls. He would say, "Oh, that I had but strength! How would I pray and sigh and cry to God for the poor world that lives in sin and pride!"

He expressed himself most pathetically to his relations when he took his leave of them.

At last, he asked what angel that was that he saw before him. "Well," said he, "I shall quickly be with Him. Come, Lord Jesus, come quickly!"

When a friend asked how he did, he said, "I am one bound for heaven. I would not have you pray for my life. I am afraid you do!"

On the day of his death, being full of pain, he said, "Jesus Christ bore more than this, and He died for me. And shall I be afraid to die and go to Him?"

Then said he, "O death, where is thy sting? O grave, where is thy victory?"

Example 6

An Extract of a letter from Southold, Long Island
April 23, 1698

I have been requested to give you this account
from the parents of a gracious child who, in all her
life, comported herself to walk in the Lord's holy
fear, and gave a great attention in hearing the Word
of God. The Lord was pleased to ripen her for
Himself, though she was but fifteen years and four
months old. Though she was young, it pleased the
Lord to put a great fear and awe upon her heart of
breaking the fifth commandment. And when she
was under the dispensation of God in sickness, it
pleased the Lord to endue her with patience to be
willing to bear His hand with all meekness. She
confessed herself to be a great sinner, and to have
sinned against a gracious God. But the Lord vouch-
safed her a strong faith to believe that He is a merciful God and willing to forgive sins, and that He had
forgiven her sins in the blood of our blessed Saviour
Jesus Christ.

Therefore, she was very willing to leave the world,
and her father and mother, having faith that she
was going to Christ. These were her own expressions
when her mother asked her if she was willing to die,
for she was too young to die. Sometime before she
died, she said she was not fit to die, but prayed unto
the Lord that He would please to fit her and make

her willing to die. "Oh," said she, "Death comes un-
awares. It comes like a thief in the night!" The Lord
granted her desire, for afterwards her mother asked
her, "My child, are you willing to die?" Her answer
was that now she was willing to die, and leave a
thousand worlds and father and mother and all to
go to Christ. She desired that the curtains might be
drawn that the light of this world might not deprive
her from beholding the brightness and the glory of
the other world. And when she saw her father and
mother weeping for her she said, "My dear father
and mother, don't mourn for me. You might well
mourn for me if I were to go into utter darkness, but
I am going to God in heaven. I long to be in the
New Jerusalem with the Lord Jesus Christ, and now I
can die."

And, lying a while in agony, when she came out
of that agony, she said,"Mother, did you not hear me
sing? I thought I was in heaven with the Lord Jesus
Christ and my grandparents and the holy angels,
and heard such melodious praises of God as I never
heard. I was very sorry I could not sing like them."
She said to her relations, "Oh, don't set your hearts
upon the world, nor look for the honors and riches
of this world. But seek first the kingdom of heaven!"

She would call upon her father to go to prayer at
the evening and say, "I cannot, I dare not, go to
sleep without it." She wished that some young people might come to her to put them in mind to consider their latter end and leave off their pride. There
came a young maid to see her, and she said to her
with tears that she should not follow the fashions of
the world, and not put off repentance to a sick bed.

Example 6   109

Yea, she spake to all those who were about her that they should not mind this world but the other world. Her mother asked her if she was not afraid to lie in the dust. But she was not thoughtful what should become of her body, believing her soul should go to God. "Mother," said she, "I could not sing here, but now I am going to sing the praises of God in heaven."

Looking on her father she said, "Oh, Father, there is no God like our God, for He is a God pardoning iniquity, transgression and sin." She said, "I wonder how you do to love to live in such a troublesome evil and sinful world. Don't you see how the judgments of God are all over the earth?" She often cried out, "Oh, Lord Jesus, come. Let thine angels come and carry me to the bosom of Abraham." This is a true relation of this gracious flower of the Lord Jesus Christ: She was an only child; her name was Bethiah, the daughter of Thomas and Mary Longworth.

The Lord raise up your heart to declare His wonderful mercies in working so graciously upon the heart of such a young flower.

That the Lord may raise up more such gracious souls in our rising generation, I remain,

Your affectionate brother,
J.S.

Example 7

*A notable passage, transcribed from the life of Mr. John Baily,
as it was related in a sermon preached on the
day of his funeral at Boston.
By Dr. Cotton Mather*

From a child he knew the Holy Scriptures. Yea, from a child he was wise unto salvation! In his very childhood, he discovered the fear of God upon his young heart, and prayer to God was one of his early exercises.

There was one very remarkable effect of it. His father was a man of a very licentious conversation—a gamester, a dancer, a very lewd company keeper. The mother of this elect vessel one day took him while he was yet a child and, calling the family together, made him to pray with them. His father coming to understand at what a rate the child had prayed with his family, it smote the soul of him with great conviction and proved the beginning of his conversion unto God. God did not leave off working on his heart until he proved one of the most eminent Christians in all that neighborhood. So he lived, so he died—a man of more than ordinary piety. And it was his manner, sometimes, to retire unto those very places of his lewdnesses where, having his little son in his company, he would pour out floods of tears in repenting prayers before the Lord.

Example 8

*Of Daniel Bradly, the son of Nathan Hester Bradly,
of Guilford, Connecticut, New England*

When the said child was about three years old, he
had one night an impression of the fears of death
which put him into crying. His mother told him if
he died, he would go to heaven; unto which he
replied he did not know how to like that place
where he should be acquainted with nobody. After
which, upon all occasions, he was inquisitive about
the state of souls after death and seemed to have real
apprehensions about it according unto, if not beyond, his capacity.

The third day of his sixth year, ague took him
and held him near three years. Some months before
his death, he had many grievous pains in which his
patience was very observable. Yet he once felt a pang
of impatience so as to think it would have been better if he had never been born, yet submitted to his
father's reproof. After this he began to be assaulted
sharply with the fears of death and manifested
strange conceptions about the world to come. He
could not see God, nor could he apprehend how he
should love God better than his parents, how God
should love him, or how he could live in heaven,
especially if his parents were not there or if he
might not know them. He also expressed difficulty
in believing the resurrection of the body, and was

continually asking his mother questions about things of this nature and how it could be, if he died and was eaten up of worms, that he could live again. She then told him the words of Job: "And though after my skin, worms destroy this body, yet in my flesh shall I see God." And if she told him anything that she heard, or the good people so apprehended or the like, it gave him little content unless she could assure him it was so in the Bible. That would always settle him down. He told his mother that he thought the reason why people read the Bible was that they might find out what God would have them to do. And they prayed for what they would have God do for them.

He was much troubled that he was not big enough to pray. His father told him that parents prayed for their children, but that did not satisfy him till it was told him he was big enough to pray for himself. But then he doubted he could pray aright. His mother told him he must pray according to his ability and God would accept it. Then he addressed himself to the duty, and would have all go out of the room except his mother. She was to stay so that, if he prayed what was not right, she might tell him. Then, with great solemnity, he fixed his eyes and asked his mother whether he should begin with that expression (Blessed God) which was not usual in the beginning of prayer in his hearing, and he, manifesting some extraordinary realizing apprehensions of God, was exceeding affecting to his mother. The substance of his prayer was that he might live and be a comfort to his parents—or, if he must die, that God would own him, love him, help

Example 8   113

him to love God, and make him know how it should
be with him in the world to come. He desired to be
willing to die when his time came. After this, he frequently was observed to pray, and desired to be alone
for that end.

One time he had great sadness fall upon him
that lasted some time before the cause of it was
known. But at last he told his mother that God was
always angry with him, and he was afraid to tell her
why till she persuaded him. Then he confessed that
he had been guilty of a lie that he told, and would
have told another if he had not some way been prevented, and that he doubted the sin of that to him
was as great as if he went through with it. His
mother asked him if he were sorry for it. He said he
was formerly sorry for it, but now more than ever.
His mother told him that, if he were sorry for it, God
would have mercy. He asked her whether it were so
in the Bible. She told him the word was, "He that
confesseth and forsaketh his sin shall find mercy."

He said he knew what confessing was, but he did
not understand forsaking. She said that it was to do
so no more. That gave him some quiet, yet still trouble and fear of God's anger hung about him. Then
his mother told him of Christ's redemption, at
which he smiled and wondered, asking whether it
was certainly so, that Christ died for man's sake. He
said he had never heard it before. She asked if he
did not remember it being read in the family or
taught in the catechism? He said he did not, but
now greatly rejoiced in the apprehension of Christ's
love so revealed.

After this he had a strong pang of temptation,

and asked his sister whether she might not kill him. His mother (being out of the room) came in and reproved him for saying so sinful a word. He asked her how it appeared to be sin, seeing he lived in so much pain. She put him in mind of Mr. [John] Cotton's explication of the sixth command, that we are not to shorten the lives of ourselves or others, but preserve both (upon which he paused a while), and then desired his mother to teach him the catechism (which he had learned before) and she did from the beginning until she came past that question of the sixth command, which he readily answered to. But then he desired to go to that which was better. She asked him what he meant. He answered, "Whereabout it speaks of the eternal Son of God."

She turned to that part of the catechism, and upon that answer, "Jesus Christ is the only Son of God, who for our sakes became man that He might redeem and save us." He lifted up his hand and said, "It is enough", and so seemed to meditate thereon.

Also it was observed that, before and after his sickness began, he had so dealt with and reproved grown persons for what he saw in them was evil (in private) that the persons themselves have confessed, that they hoped his Christian reproofs would be for their good, that they should never forget them, for in them he spoke to their consciences.

He had a desire to make a will to dispose of what he had, that he might leave it as a token of his love to his relations and other friends he had received kindness from in his sickness but would not do it until he had his father's consent, which he desired.

Example 8 115

This being granted, he disposed of those things he had (though some of them were but trifles) with as much discretion and prudent consideration as if they had been matters of the greatest moment and he a man of mature judgment. He also ordered who would dig his grave, expressed his desire to die, and was heard praying for death. He told his mother immediately before he died he was now going to heaven and that it would be best for her that he should die, for now she was forced to take a great deal of pains with him, but then he should be at rest. He asked her if she did not see it was so, and wondered at her slowness to acknowledge it. He remembered his love to his relations, thankful to those who had been often watching with him, and prayed his mother to remember them all with such tokens of his love as were in his power to give, nominating several particular persons. All this he spoke with great cheerfulness, and yet with solemnity, and so sunk down in his mother's arms and died quietly.

Example 9

Early piety exemplified in Elizabeth Butcher

Section I
Containing a brief account of her from her birth in July, 1709, to her first remarkable illness in September, 1716.

Elizabeth Butcher, daughter of Alvin and Elizabeth Butcher of Boston, was born July 14, 1709. Her parents gave her up to God from the womb, and as soon as she was capable of speaking they began to instruct her in the things of God. When she was about two and a half years old, as she lay in the cradle, she would ask herself that question, "What is my corrupt nature?" and would make answer again to herself, "It is empty of grace, bent unto sin and only to sin, and that continually." She took great delight in learning her catechism and would not willingly go to bed without saying some part of it.

She being a weak child, her mother carried her into the country for health. And, when she was about three years old, and at meetings, she would sit with her eyes fixed on the minister to the admiration of all who sat about her, who said that grown-up people might learn and take example of her. She took great delight in reading, and was ready and willing to receive instruction. But nothing more extraordinary about her appeared till she came to be

Example 9   117

about six years old. Then she began to inquire concerning God and the nature and affairs of her soul,
and she said she was afraid she had not lived up to
that end for which she was made. She was asked
what was the end she was made for. The child answered, "To glorify God, but I am afraid I have not
lived to the glory of God as I should have done." She
was then told that she must pray to God that He
would be pleased to pardon her sins and give her
grace to serve and glorify Him.

She was not contented with the bare reading of
God's Word but would frequently ask the meaning
of it. And when she was at her work, she would often
ask where such and such places of Scripture were
and would mention the words that she might be directed to find them. It was her practice to carry her
catechism or some other good book to bed with her.
In the morning, she would be sitting up in her bed
reading before any of the family were awake besides
her.

One day, as she was sitting by the fire, she asked
why eating the forbidden fruit was counted sin to
our first parents. At another time, she asked who was
meant by the wise and foolish virgins and what was
meant by the oil in the lamps. As she was reading a
sermon of Dr. Cotton Mather's, she asked who was
meant by the good cedar. And when she was told she
said, "And who are meant by the fowls that are just
mentioned?"

She was told they meant little children, and
Christ called them to come to Him. "But," said she,
"how can I, who am but a child, go to Christ?" Being
informed she said, "But will Christ accept me?" She

was answered "Yes," and several places of Scripture
were mentioned for her encouragement.

Section II
*Containing a short account of her in her first illness
from September, 1716 to February, 1717.*

In September, 1716, she was taken ill and, in her
sickness, behaved herself with such wonderful patience that all who came near admired. She would
often put up that request, "Heavenly Father, give me
Thy Christ, give me Thy grace, and pardon all my
sins for Jesus Christ's sake, Amen." Then she said,
"What is sanctification?" and made answer to herself, "It is the work of God's free grace."

"What are the benefits which in this life
accompany or flow from justification, adoption and
sanctification? They are assurance of God's love,
peace of conscience, joy in the Holy Ghost, increase
of grace, and perseverance therein to the end."

Being asked if she was willing to die and go to
Christ, she said, "Yes."

"But, child, you know you are a sinner."

She said "Yes."

"And you know where the wicked go when they
die?"

She said, "Yes, they are cast into hell."

And, being asked if she was not afraid of going
there, she said, "No, for Christ is an all-sufficient
Saviour and He is able to save me, and I hope He
will. Though I have not yet seen Christ, yet I hope I

Example 9   119

shall see him."

Awhile after she said, "I am weary of this world and long to be gone. Oh, when shall I go? Oh, when shall I go?"

Her mother asked her if she was willing to leave her here alone. She answered, "Yes, for when you die, I hope you will go to heaven too."

Feeling an alteration in herself, she desired her mother to send for Mr. [Joseph] Sewall,[1] and, when he came, he asked her how she did. She answered, "Very weak."

He asked her if she was willing to die. She said, "Yes."

He said, "Do you not know you are a sinner?"

"Yes."

He asked her if she had not heard that there was another and a better world than this. She answered, "Yes."

He asked her several other questions, but they have slipped my memory. He was about to ask her one question, but said it was a great one to ask a child, but however he would, and said to her, "Child, are you willing humbly to submit to the will of God either for life or death?"

She said, "Yes."

Awhile after she was weeping and, being asked the reason, she said, "I thought I saw the flames of hell and was going there, but I thought I saw Christ, and He called me to come to Him; and then I was not afraid. I have cried to God for grace to serve

---

[1] 1688-1769, pastor of Old South Church in Boston from 1713.

Him."

Awhile after she was taken with convulsion fits and lay several hours, all hopes of recovery were taken away. But she revived again, her pain returning with greater violence. She prayed to God to take her away out of this miserable world and cried, "O God, my God, if Thou wilt please to take me away, I will be willing to bear what pain Thou shalt please to lay upon me. Oh God, my dear God, I love Thee dearly!" And this she repeated several times over.

To her mother, sitting by her weeping, the child said, "Dear mother, you make me have more pain."

Her mother said, "No, my dear child, I don't!"

She said, "Yes, you cry, and that troubles me and causes me to have more pain."

Mr. Sewall, being sent for again, said, "Child, Is it not better to be in heaven with God and Christ than to be here?"

She answered, "Yes, yes."

He asked her if he should pray to God that He would be pleased to take her to Himself. She made a quick reply, doubling her words, "Yes, yes."

He asked her another question, but being in great trouble, it has slipped my memory. The child made no answer to it and only said, "I am spent."

A few hours after, her pains abating again, the fits returned with more violence then before, held her several hours, and then left her. She lay for some days so senseless that she did not know those who came to see her. But it pleased God to restore her again to her former health. And before she was able to sit up, she would call for her book and lie and

Example 9   121

read by the hour.

Section III
*Containing a brief account of her from her first
remarkable illness in the fall and winter,
1716, to her second in April, 1718.*

She had by course read almost through the Old
Testament, but at other times her delight was to
read in the New concerning the birth of Christ and
His sufferings; and would ask the meaning of what
she read. One day she sat by herself reading the sev-
enth chapter of Revelation concerning the number
of those who were sealed. When she came to the
ninth verse, she was overheard to weep until she
came to the end of the chapter.

One morning as she lay in her bed, she asked
what was meant by the fountain, the house of David,
and the inhabitants of Jerusalem in Zechariah 13:1.
Hearing a sermon from Luke 15 concerning the
prodigal son a few days later, she was saying the text
over to herself. She then asked who was meant by
the father and who by the son.

She had begun to learn the proofs of the
Assembly's Catchism, and when she came to 1 John
5:7 she asked if the Father was God, if the Son was
God also, and if the Holy Ghost was God also. "For it
is said here that there are three that bear record in
heaven—the Father, the Word and the Holy Ghost,
and these three are one. And this seems as if there

were three gods, and yet there is but one." She desired to be told something of this mystery and was told there was but one God, though there were three persons in the godhead. She was told that Christ was the eternal Son of God, the same in substance and equal with the Father in power and glory, and was God.

Then the child said, "Though Christ is the Son of God, yet He is God also?"

Answer was made her, "Yes," and that the Holy Ghost was the Spirit of God, proceeded both from the Father and the Son, was the same in substance with them both, and was equal in power and glory.

Awhile after, she asked if Christ took upon Him the nature of a man. She was told that He did.

She rejoiced greatly when the Lord's Day came, especially if it were fair weather for her to go to the public worship of God. And, when she came home, she would take a book and sit and read until it was time to go to the afternoon exercise, without the least sign of weariness. And, if she was detained at home on the Sabbath, she would not spend the day in idleness but in religious employments.

It pleased God to exercise her with great pain in every part of her body, which somewhat impaired the natural quickness and strength of her senses. But between two or three months before her death her understanding was brightened to admiration. When the spring came on and mention was made of the public catechizing, she rejoiced greatly and would be often speaking of its drawing near. One morning as she lay in her bed she said, "O that charming day, O that sweet day is coming!" Being

Example 9   123

asked what day she meant, she answered, "Catechizing Day, I mean that sweet day." A few days after that she said, "I won't depend upon going to catechizing, for I believe I shall be prevented by some means or other."

She was told that, if she was well and the weather permitted, nothing else would hinder her. "Ah," said the child, "I am persuaded I shall be prevented some way or other from going." And according to the strong impulse she had upon her mind, it proved to her. For she was taken sick two or three days before the catechizing came, which was in April 1718.

Section IV
Containing a more particular account of her in her second illness from April 1718, to June succeeding, when she died.

When she was first taken, she was in some doubt of her spiritual state and said she was afraid she did not belong to God nor love Him as she should. "For, Mother, you have told me that they who fear God and love Him make it their chief care and endeavor to keep His commandments. But I am afraid I have not kept them as I ought." Her mother asked her what particular command she would accuse herself of breaking. She said, "The fifth commandment says, 'Honor thy father and thy mother,' and have I honored you? Have I obeyed you as I ought?"

Her mother told her, "You have been an obedient child to me, and where you have offended in any small matter I forgive you and pray God to forgive you also."

The day following she cried out, "I am a great sinner, a great sinner. What will become of me, oh, what will become of me? I am afraid that God will not have mercy on me. My sins are so many and so great." She was told that, though her sins were ever so great and many, yet the mercy of God was greater and more abundant than her sins, for that, like Himself, is infinite and endures forever. She was told that there was forgiveness with Him that he might be feared, and He had promised that those who confess and forsake their sins should find mercy. But said the child, "Satan tempts me to despair of mercy because my sins are so great and many." But she was then exhorted not to give way to the temptations of Satan but to hope in the mercy of God. "For the Lord taketh pleasure in them that fear Him, and in them that hope in His mercy." And she was told that He said in Isaiah 55:7, "Let the wicked forsake his way, and the unrighteous man his thoughts, and let him return unto the Lord, and He will have mercy upon him, and to our God. For He will abundantly pardon."

Awhile later she said, "Behold I was shapen in iniquity, and in sin did my mother conceive me. I am a miserable and sinful creature. Convinced I am of sin, but afraid not converted. I am a poor creature who has no sight of my interest in Christ, and without a Christ, without a Christ, I am undone forever. Oh, for a Christ! Oh, for a Christ to save me!" And then she prayed and said:

"Lord, have mercy on me according to Thy lov-

Example 9   125

ingkindness. According to the multitude of Thy tender mercies, blot out all my transgressions with Thine own blood. Wash me throughly from mine iniquities, and cleanse me from my sins. Create in me a clean heart, O God, and renew a right spirit within me! Oh, give me a new heart, a humble heart, a broken heart, and a contrite spirit! Oh, sanctify me by Thy Holy Spirit throughout, in soul, spirit, and body! Renew me in the whole man after Thine own image in knowledge, righteousness, and true holiness. Oh, give me a Christ, give me Thy grace, and pardon all my sins! O Lord, take away all my iniquity and receive me graciously! Circumcise my heart to fear Thy name and lead me in the way that is pleasing in Thy sight.

"Oh, be my God in life, my Guide unto death, and the unchangeable portion of my soul forever! Fit and prepare me for all changes, but especially for death, my great and last change. And this I beg for Thy Son Jesus Christ's sake, Amen."

In the time of her health, she was very careful of her words and no ill language was ever heard to proceed from her lips. Yet, now, in her sickness, she examined what sins she had been guilty of, both in words and actions. And taking a view of the commandments, some of them she said she was afraid she had been guilty of breaking, accused herself of disobedience, and condemned herself for her sins, "Now I am suffering the desert of my sins. Oh, that I might have but a moment's ease. But I need not wonder that I have no ease, for I deserve none. Have mercy upon me, O Lord, for I am weak. O Lord, heal me, for my bones are sore vexed. Look upon my afflictions and my pain, and forgive all my sins."

Mr. [Thomas] Prince[2] came in to see her. She desired him to pray with her. He asked her what he should pray for. She answered that God would be pleased to pardon all her sins and give her an interest in Christ.

Awhile after she cried out, "Oh, I am a poor creature that lacks assurance. Oh, for assurance! Oh, for assurance! Oh, that God would be pleased to lift up the light of His countenance upon me! Oh, that He would be pleased to own me in His covenant and bless me!" Her mother seeing her in this distress asked her if she should send for Mr. Sewall to talk with him and hear what he had to say to her. The child answered, "Mr. Sewall may give me encouragement as you do, but unless God speaks to me too, all will signify nothing."

"Well, child," said her mother, "wait upon God still, who will in His own time, I hope, speak peace to your soul." Mr. Sewall was sent for, but he was not at home.

She was told for her encouragement that she was a lamb of Christ's flock, and that He had said He would take the lambs in His arms and carry them in His bosom; and "Suffer little children to come unto me, and forbid them not, for of such is the kingdom of heaven." And you know that promise in Proverbs 8:17, "I love them that love me, and those that seek me early shall find me."

The child answered, "If the Lord is pleased to

---

[2] 1687-1758, Sewall's colleague at Old South Church from 1718.

Example 9   127

help me, I will seek Him." She was told that the Lord would help her, and she was exhorted to trust in the free grace and mercy of God through Christ. "Oh," said the child, "I am willing to accept Christ, but I am afraid Christ is not willing."

Answer was made that, if she was willing to accept Christ, that, to be sure, Christ was willing to accept her. She answered, "I am willing." A while later she said, "I will venture my soul upon Christ, and if I perish, Lord, it shall be at the fountain of Thy mercy. For Thou hast promised that whosoever cometh unto Thee, Thou wilt in no wise cast out. Oh, Lord, I desire as I am able to come unto Thee, and I am sure Thou wilt not cast me off." She was then composed for some time.

But Satan assaulted her again, in setting her sins before her, and she cried out, "Oh the sin of my nature! Unless my soul is sprinkled with the blood of Christ, it is enough to undo me were I guilty of no other."

About a month before her death, on the Sabbath afternoon, she said to her mother, "Now I have a believing sight of Christ. Now Christ is mine, and I am His. Oh, how sweet is Christ! Oh, He is sweet; He is sweet! And if you but tasted and felt what I do, you would long to be gone." Then she said, "Come, Lord Jesus, come quickly. Dear Jesus, sweet Jesus, come quickly."

Then she said, "Lord Jesus, give me patience. Give me patience to wait Thy time, for Thy time is the best time. Lord Jesus, give me patience." Her mother sat weeping by her. To comfort her, the child said, "Dear mother, though we part now, it will be but a little while before you will follow and come to me, and that will be a happy meeting for us, to meet at the right hand of Christ in the Great Day." Then she thanked her mother for the instructions and corrections she had given her and said, "Had it not been for them, I might have gone to hell. But it won't be long now before the blessed angels will come and carry my soul to the bosom of Christ. Oh, I long to be gone. I long to be gone to that blessed place. Sweet Lord Jesus, come quickly."

A while later she said, "My pain is great which I undergo to go to Christ, but not so great as the pains Christ underwent for me. Oh, I wonder, I wonder that Christ should be so willing to die for me, who am so great a sinner." Mr. Sewall was sent for again but, before he came, the child was so spent with extreme pain and much speaking that she was not able to say anything to him. In the night, she asked the young woman who watched with her to read the 25th chapter of Matthew to her. One morning she asked, "Where is that place of Scripture, 'Eat, O friends; drink, yea drink abundantly, O beloved'?" The hourglass standing on the table, she asked to have it turned and said, "My glass is almost run. My work is almost ended."

On Thursday, three weeks before her death, her mother, feeling an alteration in her, said, "My child is struck with death." Upon which she replied, "Is death come, and am I prepared? Am I prepared?" She lay still for some time and then said, "O death, where is thy sting? O grave, where is thy victory, and what will you gain by this thing?"

There was a person she had a peculiar respect for

Example 9   129

and desired her mother, when she had opportunity, to speak to her. For she was afraid she did not consider her soul and eternity.

The Lord's Day following she said the 23rd Psalm, and when she had concluded it her mother asked her if she was not afraid to pass through the dark valley of the shadow of death. She answered, "No, for God has promised that He will never leave me nor forsake me, neither will He suffer me to leave or forsake Him."

Lying in great pain day and night, she would often say, "Lord Jesus, give me patience that I may not dishonor God." She said, "Oh, if I should be deceived at last, and deceive others, and they think I am good! Oh, how miserable shall I be forever?"

Her aunt Stone being present, and the child being in great pain and complaining of those about her for refusing to do something for her which she found relieved her, as they were fearful of overdoing, she said, "They do not pity me, but I hope Christ pities me and will prepare a place for me." A little while later, being restless with her pains, she checked herself, saying, "Why do I complain? Christ endured more than this for me. I wonder how He bore it?" And a little while later, hearing it thunder, she said, "It thunders. I am afraid God will kill me with it. But whether he kills me with that or with his pain, if I may but go to Christ it will be well."

The Tuesday following, Mr. Sewall came to see her. After some discourse, he asked her on what she depended for salvation. She replied, "On Christ and the promises."

He said, "Well, child, hold fast your faith and still

trust in Christ."

Then she said, "Oh, I long to go to that blessed place!"

He asked her what blessed place. She not readily answering, he said, "Do you mean heaven?"

She answered, "Yes." And, when he was going away, she desired him to remember her in his prayers and asked him when he would come again to see her.

Two persons being in the room, they said to one another, "This child has been a child of affliction all its days."

The child replied, "And it is for my good."

She had another combat with Satan, and said he would persuade her that Christ was withdrawn from her. She cried out, "Oh, what shall I do? Oh, what shall I do? I am undone! Oh, Lord, cast me not out of Thy sight. Cast me not away from Thy presence and take not Thy Holy Spirit from me. Restore unto me the joy of Thy salvation and uphold me with Thy free spirit. Neither leave me nor forsake me, but guide me by Thy counsel while here, and afterwards receive me to Thine heavenly kingdom. And this I ask for Thy Son Jesus Christ's sake, and in testimony of my desires and assurance to be heard, I say Amen."

She was comforted again in the night. The watcher sitting by her bedside about midnight heard her say, "Yonder, yonder, up above, sits my Saviour, clothed in love. And there's my smiling God."

She said she had something to say to Mr. Sewall the next time he should come to see her. Being

Example 9   131

asked what it was, she said she would thank him for the many prayers he put up for her, for God had heard and answered them. At another time she said concerning Christ, "Why is His chariot so long in coming? Why do the wheels of His chariot stay so long? For me to stay is pain; but to die is gain."

Mr. Prince, coming to see her the Monday before her death, she desired him to pray with her. He said, "Well, and what shall we pray for now?"

She replied, "That I may have a saving knowledge of Christ, that God would be pleased to pardon all my sins and prepare me for death, my great and last change."

The day following, her pains abated and she seemed to be better for two or three days. No one perceived her to draw near her change until, a few minutes before she was taken speechless, the child said something choked her. Her mother felt her hands. Finding them in a cold sweat and her countenance altered, she said, "My child is going."

"Ah, Mother," said the child, "So must you as well as I." She said something more, but her speech and spirits failing we could not understand her.

She breathed her soul into the arms of Christ on Friday, the 13th of June, 1718, being eight years and just eleven months old.

Example 10

Mistress Abiel Goodwin, who died at Boston,
October 3, 1727, in the 20th year of her age.

Her father died a very young man, but in so uncommon and victorious a manner that an account is already published of it in Dr. Cotton Mather's *Coelestinus.*[1] She was born after the death of her father, and for that cause the name of Abiel (or, God my Father) was given her.

This young person was one who began quickly to take the yoke of her Saviour upon her—yea, so quickly and with such gracious dawns of piety that she knew not the time of her first coming into the life of God. And God forbid that we should rashly pass the doom of the unregenerate on all who are, and very many of the newborn, we hope, are so circumstanced.

Under the influences of a pious education, she was, from her childhood, used to the religion of the closet, afraid of doing anything that the light of God in her young soul did not allow. She was courteous, affable, full of benignity, ready to do good offices for all about her, accompanied and advantaged with a discretion which was an agreeable varnish

---

[1] Cotton Mather published his Coelestinus: *A Conversation in Heaven, Quickened and Assisted, with Discoveries of Things in the Heavenly World* in 1723.

Example 10   133

upon all.

Her attendance on the means of grace was very diligent. Among the rest, she constantly attended the weekly lectures and lamented the scandal that those precious opportunities were so shamefully neglected in a city where a worldly mind so evidently governed the inhabitants.

Hereby she came to live by the faith of the Son of God and His everlasting love to her, so that the dread of death was nobly conquered in her. In the year 1721, when the small pox carried off so many hundreds in the city of Boston, she declared unto her widowed mother that unless God had service for her to do, more particularly in being very helpful to her, she would have chosen then to have left a world that she saw full of little but sin and vanity.

Her illness began upon her when she was little more than 16 years of age, and she was confined to the house for two years before she died. Hereby she was prevented from the execution of a purpose that her young heart was earnestly set upon, which was to have approached the Holy Table in the way of the gospel and of our churches, to have made her claim to the sacrifice of her Saviour, and set her seal to the covenant of salvation, according to His institution there. She greatly lamented that, though she were so very young, she had not publicly done what she had proposed, of giving herself up unto the Lord among his people. But she said, "I have done it secretly a thousand times, and the Lord has accepted my willing mind. And what fault there might be in my delay, He has assured me that he has pardoned it." But how earnestly she urged upon her young friends the serious and speedy discharge of their plain duty. "Do this. The omission whereof forever, where the conscience is not seared, makes an uneasy deathbed."

At length she became confined to the bed for 18 weeks altogether. She expressed a strong belief that she would find extraordinary supports provided for her, and she found them. She found them to astonishment. She had now fallen into an dropsy-like condition. In this time, though many wearisome nights were appointed for her, yet she did not possess months of vanity. She did good all the while and brought much of the fruit by which her heavenly Father has been and will be glorified.

In these months, the first thing that I took notice of was the zeal, flame, and ardor wherewith she addressed her lively exhortations to those who visited her to make haste unto their Savior, into a life of piety, to make sure of and lay hold on eternal life. She did not offer her exhortations of this importance unto older people very much, for, she said, she did not count it good manners for her to do the part of a monitor to those who were much older than herself. But with younger people she was inexpressibly in earnest that they would now, even today, hear the voice of God, remember their Creator, and have no rest, give no sleep to their eyes nor slumber to their eyelids, until they had got into the covenant of God their Saviour and yielded themselves unto the Lord, resolving to be the Lord's.

As a wise winner of souls, how sweetly she invited them, "Oh, come and sit under the shadow of your Saviour! Sweet, sweet you will find His fruit unto you." Great numbers of younger people came to her,

Example 10   135

and she not only very importunately but also very particularly expostulated with them about their delay to make thorough work of that conversion to God and resort to the wings of the Saviour, which was infinitely necessary in order to their dying in safety and with comfort. She took several by the hand, vehemently urging them to consent unto the proposal of the covenant of life and resign and engage themselves unto their Savior. She would not let go of their hands until they declared unto her that they did so. She pleaded with some of them, "God spared you in the time of the great mortality six years ago. He has come twice three years, looking for fruit. But, oh, what fruit has he found upon you?" And in some whom she saw things amiss, it was very affecting to see how lovingly but how faithfully and how solemnly she dispensed reproofs unto them. The hammers were enough to have broken rocks to pieces.

In this time, as it sometimes is with souls who are getting loose from the flesh and have gotten very far on towards the invisible world, she had some unaccountable impressions upon her mind relating to things not commonly coming under human cognizance. There were surprising instances, not so proper to be now and here spoken of. But there is one I would speak of because it may be a little subservient unto the main design which I am now to prosecute.

In her inculcations of it upon young people, that they would immediately come under the yoke of their Saviour and so be prepared for a death which they knew not how suddenly might overtake them, she said, "Mind what I say. You shall see sudden deaths, I say, sudden deaths, quickly multiplied among you. Young as well as old shall be reached with them." It was not long, but a very few weeks after this prediction before she was able to observe, "Well, there have been 14 sudden deaths which you have seen dispensed since my speaking to you. But I am to tell you there will be many more than these."

But from this I cannot but go on to take notice of the prospect that her Saviour gave her of the heaven that she now saw open to receive her, and the heavenly peace and joy which the bright prospect filled her with. It was unspeakably edifying unto us to see so young a person, one of 19, so rejoicing in hope of the glory of God—yea, rejoicing with a joy unspeakable and full of glory.

In this time when one, to treat her with a term suiting her ingenuity, told her that, considering the nature of her malady, her condition might be called a going to heaven by water. Anon she would be able to sing unto her Saviour that song of the redeemed, "He sent from above. He took me. He drew me out of many waters." Her answer was, "Water, yea, and if I should go to heaven by fire too, I am sure heaven would compensate for all the trouble of it. Oh, lovely, lovely, lovely to be there! How I long to be there." Then she would break out, "Oh, that I had the wings of a dove. Then I would fly away unto Him and be at rest." And again, "Oh, why is His chariot so long in coming? Why tarry the wheels of His chariot?" But she corrected it, "I will wait, for He who will come will come, and will not tarry."

And she said, "Oh, what shall I find in Mount

Example 10   137

Zion, the city of the living God, the heavenly Jerusalem?"

She said that for some time, though she knew it would be well with her, yet she was at a loss, and did not know how her departed soul would apprehend things in the other world to which it was now going. But when her thoughts were one day full of perplexity about the matter, she thought she heard a voice distinctly say to her, "Be satisfied. Thy departing soul shall immediately pass into a wonderful glory. Thy poor body also shall still remain united unto thy Redeemer, and it shall be after some time restored unto thy soul with wondrous glory. Therein thou shalt forever glorify Him who has redeemed thee."

The Scriptures being so set in this light unto her, she broke forth into raptures, "Oh, wonderful! Oh, wonderful! Am I so near unto a wondrous glory? And this vile body too united to my Saviour, and regarded by Him. Oh, grace! grace! Oh, free grace! Oh, rich grace! I shall glorify thee for evermore." It was a frequent exclamation with her, "Oh, the grace of the glorious Rock of Ages! I have everlasting strength in that glorious Rock of Ages."

She said, upon her being asked her choice in the matter, "I would rather die, were it the will of God, if it were for nothing but this: If I live I shall sin, and I would rather die than sin. But if it be the will of God that I should live, I am willing to live and suffer anything that He shall be pleased to order for me. It will be nothing to what my Saviour suffered for me, the chief of sinners."

She often fell into fits, which were attended with

an extremity of pains.

But at her first coming out of them, her first words were usually such as one might have expected from one who had been caught up into paradise. They were "Hallelujah! Oh! Salvation to our God who sitteth on the throne, and unto the Lamb. Oh, blessing and glory and honor be unto our God forever and ever!" She said, "Oh, welcome fits! Oh, welcome pains! Oh, welcome anything that will bring me nearer to Christ!" She said, "Well, the more I bear, the more I love! The more I suffer from the wise and good hand of my Saviour, the more I love Him!"

Her mother wiping the sweat off her face, hereupon she said, "O my mother, 'tis not like the drops of blood which my Saviour shed for me, a miserable sinner."

One with some compassion said, "Poor creature!"

She replied, "Oh, do not call me so. I am a rich creature, for the blood of the Son of God has cleansed me from all my sins and His unsearchable riches are mine!"

Another used the term of "Distressed creature!"

Upon that she said, "No, say 'Happy creature.' "

She lay awake with her eyes closed a long time altogether. Being at length asked what she was doing, she replied, "I am thinking, thinking, what that heaven is which I am going to. Thinking how they are employed in heaven. I now know a little of that. Thinking what shall be my first word when I come to heaven."

Being asked what it should be, she an-

Example 10   139

swered,"What? Hallelujah! Hallelujah! Oh, the free and rich grace which has brought me here! Oh, my Saviour, what, what, shall I render to Thee!"

Coming to speak about the matchless glories of her Saviour, she said, "I have read and heard His name is Wonderful. Oh! I did not understand the meaning of that word. But now I have some understanding of it. I heard and read He is altogether lovely. Oh, I did not know the meaning of that word, but now I know something of it."

Once a temptation assaulted her that a devil would make a prey of her departing soul. But she soon answered and vanquished it, saying, "No, no, my Saviour won't let Satan pluck me out of His powerful and merciful hand. Satan, when my hour comes, my flight will be too nimble for you."

Hereupon she expressed in very extraordinary terms how welcome her death had become unto her. It came to her as one who comes to take off the yoke and give food to the weary. Being asked if she were not frightened at it she replied, "Frightened? No, my Saviour has made it a better friend to me than any I have in the world. Oh, my friend, how welcome, how welcome to me!"

The tolling of funeral bells even transported her to think what joys the like toll for her would proclaim her to be gone to. And she sent messages unto some sick people in the neighborhood, that they should not be afraid of dying but repair to the glorious Christ that she had repaired to. They should find Him full of grace, full of love. The comforter that should relieve their souls would not be far from them. She therewith declared that there was one word which the Spirit of God had made worth a thousand worlds, even that word, "Our light affliction here, which is but for a moment, works for us a far more exceeding, and eternal weight of glory."

But now I must own that, though her hope in her death was what appeared very amiable to me and very delectable, yet there was one thing that appeared much more so, and this was her being willing to live.

Though she so wished for death, and had such assurance that the hour of her death would be the best hour that ever she saw; and though the distemper which excruciated her had much sorrow and anguish in it; and as by and by her expiration she was assured of the Lord sending to take her and draw her out of deadly waters, yet with a most profound submission, she was willing to wait God's time for the deliverance. Her will was admirably swallowed up in the will of her God. Her cry was continually, "The will of the Lord be done."

How often she comforted herself, "Heaven, heaven will make amends for all the pains that I undergo in my passage to it!" How often did she compose herself, "If I may do good unto any one soul by my staying here, or if I do no more good than this, that the sight of my pain shall teach any to be thankful to God for their health and ease, this alone will make amends for all my misery."

She would often speak of sufferings for Christ and say, "Oh, what a pleasure it would be unto me to be burned to death for Him." And sufferings from Christ, she often said, she could bear with pleasure because they came from Him. Anything from his

Example 10   141

hand, she said, "Oh! 'Tis a pleasure to take it."

Thus patience had its perfect work. Being asked how she did, she answered, "Oh, better and better. That is to say, nigher and nigher to heaven."

A little before she died, being asked whether her comfort continued, she said, "Yes, oh, more than ever! But I am so weak that I cannot express the joy I feel. I long more than ever to be gone. You may now look for my death every minute." Some of her last words were, "I have now finished the work that my God has ordered for me." So she kept waiting for the mercy stroke which soon released her.

Selected Bibliography

[Many of these works are not written from an evangelical viewpoint, but they do provide useful information when read with caution.]

Adair, John. *The Founding Fathers: The Puritans in England and America.* Grand Rapids: Baker Book House, 1986.

Adams, Jay. *The Biblical View of Self-Esteem, Self-Love, Self-Image.* Eugene: Harvest House Publishers, 1986.

Baxter, Richard. *The Practical Works of Richard Baxter.* 4 vols., Ligonier: Soli Deo Gloria, 1990-1991.

Bushnell, Horace. *Christian Nurture.* Introduction by Luther Weigle. New Haven: Yale University Press, 1967.

Darton, F. J. Harvey. *Children's Books in England.* New York: Cambridge University Press, 1960.

Demers, Patricia. *Heaven Upon Earth: The Form of Moral and Religious Children's Literature to 1850.* Knoxville: University of Tennessee Press, 1993.

Fleming, Sandford. *Children and Puritanism.* New York: Arno Press, 1969.

Foxe, John. *Foxe's Christian Martyrs of the World.* Westwood: Barbour and Company, 1985.

Haller, William. *Foxe's Book of Martyrs and the Elect Nation.* London: J. Cape, 1963.

Hambrick-Stowe, Charles E. *The Practice of Piety: Puritan Devotional Disciplines in the Seventeenth Century New England.* Chapel Hill: University of North Carolina Press, 1982.

Haviland, Virginia, and Coughlan, Margaret N.. *Yankee Doodle's Literary Sampler of Prose, Poetry, and Pictures.* New York: Thomas Y. Crowell, 1974.

Hendley, George. *A Memorial for Children; being an authentic account of the Conversion, Experience, and Happy Deaths of Eighteen Children.* New Haven: Sidney's Press, 1806.

Hodge, Charles. "Bushnell on Christian Nurture," *Biblical Repertory and Princeton Review,* XIX (1847), 502-539.

Hodge, Charles. *Systematic Theology.* 3 vols. Grand Rapids: William B. Eerdmans, 1975.

Janeway, James. *A Token for Children.* Introduction by Robert G. Miner Jr., New York: Garland Publications, 1977.

Janeway, James. *A Token for Children,* and Mather, Cotton. *A Token for the Children of New England.*

Boston: Z. Fowle, 1771.

Kiefer, Monica. *American Children Through their Books: 1700-1835*. Philadelphia: University of Pennsylvania Press, 1948.

Lystad, Mary. *From Dr. Mather to Dr. Seuss: 200 Years of American Books for Children*. Boston: G.K. Hall and Co., 1980.

Martin, Hugh. *Puritanism and Richard Baxter*. London: SCM Press, 1954.

Mather, Cotton. *The Great Works of Christ in America (Magnali Christi Americana)*. 2 vols. Carlisle: Banner of Truth, 1979.

Meigs, Cornelia; Eaton, Ann Thaxter; Nesbitt, Elizabeth; and Viguers, Ruth Hill. *A Critical History of Children's Literature*. New York: The MacMillan Company, 1969.

Middlekauff, Robert. *The Mathers: Three Generations of Puritan Intellectuals: 1596-1728*. New York: Oxford University Press, 1971.

Morgan, Edmund S. *The Puritan Family*. New York: Harper and Row, 1966.

Morgan, Edmund S. *Visible Saints: The History of a Puritan Idea*. Ithaca: Cornell University Press, 1974.

Myers, A.J. Wm. *Horace Bushnell and Religious Education.*
Boston: Manthorne and Burack, 1937.

Neve, J.J., and Heick, O.W. *A History of Protestant
Thought.* vol. 2: *History of Protestant Theology.* Philadelphia: The Muhlenberg Press, 1946.

Packer, James I. *A Quest for Godliness: The Puritan Vision
of the Christian Life.* Wheaton, IL: Crossway Books,
1990.

Ryken, Leland. *Worldly Saints: The Puritans as They
Really Were.* Grand Rapids: Zondervan Publishing
House, 1986.

Ryle, John Charles. *The Duties of Parents.* Choteau:
Christian Heritage Publishers, 1983.

Sloane, William. *Children's Books in England and
America in the Seventeenth Century.* New York: King's
Crown, 1955.

Stout, Harry S. *The New England Soul: Preaching and
Religious Culture in Colonial New England.* New York:
Oxford University Press, 1986.

Sutherland, Zena, and Arbuthnot, Mary. *Children and
Books.* Glenview: Scott Foresman and Company, 1986.

Swinnock, George. *The Works of George Swinnock,* 5
vols., Carlisle: Banner of Truth, 1992.

Tennent, Gilbert. *A Persuasive to the Right Use of the Passions in Religion.* Philadelphia: W. Dunlap, 1760.

Towns, Elmer L., ed. *A History of Religious Educators.* Grand Rapids: Baker Book House, 1975.

Townsend, John Rowe. *An Outline of English-Language Children's Literature.* New York: J.B. Lippincott, 1983.

Tyler, Bennet. *Letters to the Rev. Horace Bushnell, D.D., Containing Strictures on His Book, entitled "Views of Christian Nurture, and of Subjects Adjacent Thereto".* Hartford: Brown and Parsons, 1848.

Welch, d'Alte A. *A Bibliography of American Children's Books Printed Prior to 1821.* Worcester: American Antiquarian Society and Barre Publishers, 1972.

Wendell, Barrett. *Cotton Mather.* New York: Chelsea House, 1980

Wileman, William. ed. *Lambs Safely Folded.* Choteau: Gospel Mission Press, 1980.